Designer's
Design

46 remarkable contemporary pioneers
in the field of interior design and their
best works.

Designer's Design

All works reproduced in this book © Gap Japan, Co., Ltd.
Publisher: Yoshiaki Yanada
Editor: Yoshimi Takahashi
Design: Kazuko Fukada
Editorial cooperator: Zero First Design, Kazuhisa Sadokawa

First published in Japanese edition in 2006 by:
© Gap Japan, Co., Ltd.
3–9–12, Higashi, Shibuya–Ku, Tokyo 150–0011 Japan
Tel: 0081–3–5778–7170
Fax: 0081–3–5766–6401

First published in English editon in 2007 by:
© Azur Corporation

Distributed by:
AZUR Corporation (Worldwide except China)
5F Aikusu Building, 1–44–8, Jimbo–Cho, Kanda Chiyoda–ku, Tokyo 101–0051 Japan
Tel: 0081–3–3292–7601
Fax: 0081–3–3292–7602
E–mail: azur@galaxy.ocn.ne.jp
http://www.azurbook.co.jp

Beijing Designer Books Co., Ltd.(China)
Building No. 2, Desheng Office Building, No. 3, Babukou, Gulouxi Road, Xicheng
District, Beijing, P. R. China
Tel: 0086–10–6406–7653 (Beijing)   0086–21–5596–7639 (Shanghai)
     0086–22–2341–1250 (Tianjin)   0086–571–8884–8576 (Hangzhou)
     0086–27–5920– 8457 (Wuhan)   0086–20–8756–5010 (Guangzhou)
     0086–25–5807–5096 (Nanjing)   0086–755–8825–0425 (Shenzhen)
     0086–28–8660–1680 (Chengdu)
Fax: 0086–10–6406–0931
E–mail: info@designerbooks.net
Http://www.designerbooks.net

Printed in China

ISBN: 978–4–903233–23–9

CONTENTS

Epoch–making explorers for the 21st century

006   STUDIO JOB

016   Piet Hein Eek

022   Maarten Baas

030   Simon Heijdens

034   Arik Levy

044   Yves Béhar

046   Johannes Norlander

050   Jean–Marie Massaud

054   India Mahdavi

058   Eric Gizard

064   Laurent Massaloux

068   Joris Laarman

072   Frank Tjepkema

078   Koichiro Kimura

082   Ineke Hans

086   Nendo

090   Chris Kabel

Eye–catching new generation of designers

096   COMMITTEE

098   Stuart Haygarth

100   5.5 designers

106   Emiko Oki

108   Wieki Somers

112   Afke Golsteijn

118   Ted Noten

120   Wataru Komachi

124   Pernilla Jansson

126   Design Dessert

130   defyra

132   Monica Förster

138   Thomas Bernstrand

142   Todd Bracher

Epoch–making stars that continue making legends

150   Fernando+Humberto Campapna

154   Tom Dixon

162   Patricia Urquiola

170   Marcel Wanders

178   Claesson Koivisto Rune

190   Ronan & Erwan Bouroullec

198   Alfredo Haberli

206   Hella Jongerius

210   Carlo Colombo

216   Tei Syuwa

220   Björn Dahlström

226   Jasper Morrison

232   Philippe Starck

240   Ron Arad

248   Antonio Citterio

148   Column

The design in the times without maesrto
——Kaoro Tashiro

254   INDEX

255   Data Source/Enquiry

Greetings

The 20th century witnessed the flourishing and rapid development of "design". In those colorful times, people pursued a material life assiduously. Consequently, it brought about the birth of new functions and design successively, which we had never seen before. But such ardent desire would never be satisfied. What people were longing for was the "Times of Design". The 21st century that we live in inherits the wealth of 20th century. Though enjoying sufficient material means, people always feel slightly bored. Ultimately, it is design that cures us. People would not survive if they could not find the variation and value of surroundings. What is the design pursued in the present times? This question inspired me to write this book. The book illustrates the designers and artists who are active on the interior design scene as well as their works. Through this window, we can obtain a general view of those designers and artists. Their thinking, exploration, mode of expression, and their approach to design, are what we need to understand.

Epoch-making explorers for the 21st century

STUDIO JOB
Piet Hein Eek
Maarten Baas
Simon Heijdens
Arik Levy
Yves Béhar
Johannes Norlander
Jean-Marie Massaud
India Mahdavi
Eric Gizard
Laurent Massaloux
Joris Laarman
Frank Tjepkema
Koichiro Kimura
Ineke Hans
nendo
Chris Kabel

"Never to be limited to the concept of design itself" is an attempt to new approach. That is to say, to make new creation amazing the world. The significance and message conveyed could touch us deeply. These could let us re–discover both the splendid achievement and the flaw of the works in the 20th century. Either the new leaders of 21st century or the core of their design works are all around this theme. Putting aside the 20th century which brought innovation to the field of design, they are creating a new history.

STUDIO JOB

Job Smeets and Nynke Tynagel established the de-sign duo in 1998. Both of them graduated from Eind-hoven University. Now they are mainly working in Bellkey and Antwerp.

They are not only the designers from Holland, but also the designers from Europa. As European designers, they are active in extensive fields such as fashion, art and interior design, etc and attract the attention from the whole world.

Their imagination is rich and profound, which is be-yond the reach of ordinary people. Their works of art derived from such imagination are imbued with indi-vidual appeal. They design unique works, publica-tions, installations, interior and public spaces, which only are their basic designs. They clearly know that they are the treasure of inspiration. What they did is just to select and present the exact ideas which occur to their minds. The peculiar shape and size of their works present an unreal world, which embodies their belief in design. Such designs frame and illustrate the changeful free thoughts.

Starting with unique story and concept, their designs portray the great art in the history with their own man-ner. Adopting the unrealistic approach from materials and scale, they are continuously conceiving the un-precedented and marvelous designs. They make the real model in their studio, and produce works in limited amount. So that, the art could last for about a hundred years. They will continue to carry on with their concept of international design for design and art.

Art and irony, a group of humorous and charming geniuses of the touch design

STUDIO JOB
Job Smeets: Born 1970 Nynke Tynagel: Born 1977, in Netherlands

The impact art rises from the matching of the massiness and the broad–brush of bronze

"Rock Sofa & Chair"
The series of works derived from the concept of rock–digging
The bronze processed with the techniques of polishing and spray–painting, etc
together with the color variation of white and silver.

1

2

STUDIO JOB

3

4

6

5

1. "Containers"
Bronze container. It is quite interesting that the humorous shape combines with the material of superior texture absonantly.

2. "Craft"
This also belongs to the series of bronze craftworks. The objects include clock, wine glass, plant and hammer, etc.

3. "Bronze series - Ring"
The inspiration comes from the hereditary ring of Pope. There is a dead bird on one side and a "Candle man" in the appearance of baby on the other side in the work. As the highlight of the work, the green stone is also made of bronze.

4. "Bronze series - Diamond"
This work is one of the wares which are made based on the designer's personal concept of castle. The diamond is the sole treasure in the castle and the jewelry box is changed into a work of art.

5. "Bronze series - Arrow"
According to the old legend, gold arrow never misses the target. The arrow hanging on the wall is about to fly away from the bowstring.

6. "Bronze series - Knife"
It is the sole weapon in the castle. The bronze sword and axe are molded into works of art.

1

2

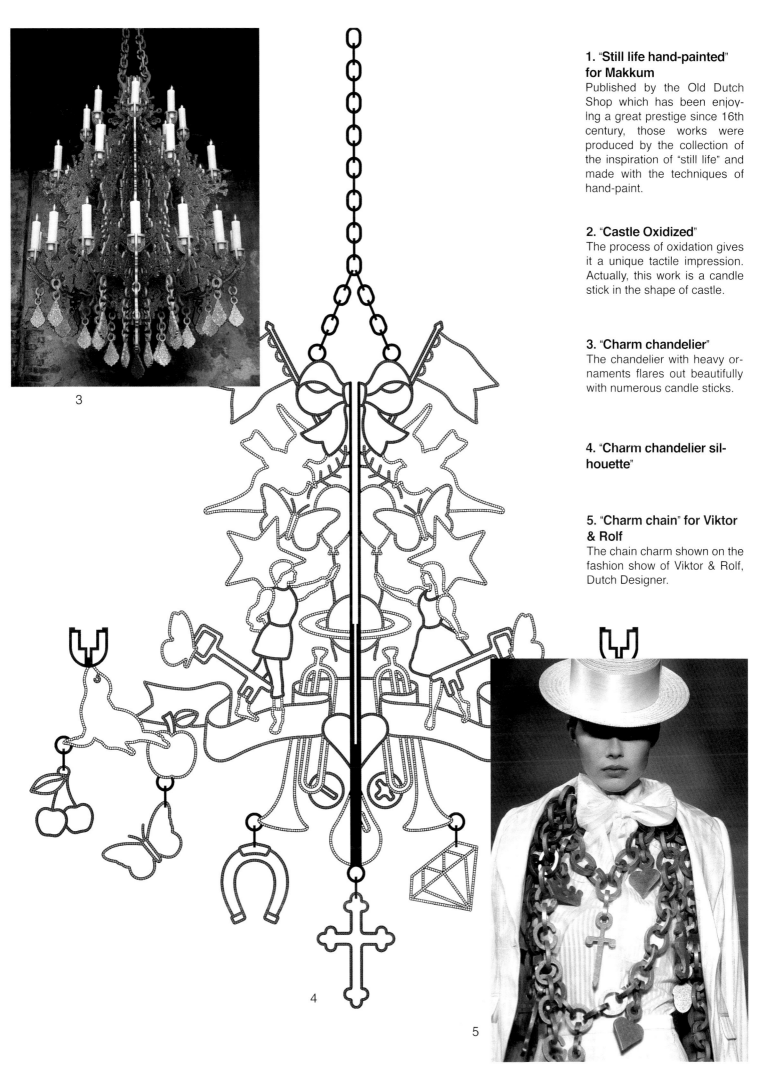

1. "Still life hand-painted" for Makkum

Published by the Old Dutch Shop which has been enjoy-Ing a great prestige since 16th century, those works were produced by the collection of the inspiration of "still life" and made with the techniques of hand-paint.

2. "Castle Oxidized"

The process of oxidation gives it a unique tactile impression. Actually, this work is a candle stick in the shape of castle.

3. "Charm chandelier"

The chandelier with heavy ornaments flares out beautifully with numerous candle sticks.

4. "Charm chandelier silhouette"

5. "Charm chain" for Viktor & Rolf

The chain charm shown on the fashion show of Viktor & Rolf, Dutch Designer.

3

4

5

1

2

3

4

1. "Bronze series – Candle man"

This candle man is the one that appeared as a baby in the work of "Ring" on page 9. According to old legend, the clumsy turtle has another identity of man who appears in various works with different shapes.

2. "Bronze series - Clock"

The design of this piece was influenced by the desk clock which was placed on the French fireplace in 1785. It is shaped of bronze in the mould made of paper and paste-board. The work was designed according to the original desk clock that was collected by the Wallace, a famous company in London. The tails of two monkeys symbolize the Logomark of the Chanel.

3. "Bronze series - Center-piece"

"Candle man" climbs up the side of Centerpiece.

4. "Bronze series - Plate"

Initially, this piece is shaped of bronze in waxen mould, which depicts the brambly forest in "overgrown with rose" and the galloping fleet of roaches which were damaging the forest. The tails of monkeys made the shape of logomark fighting against "Pretze". The central pattern shows a robot protecting fruits.

STUDIO JOB

1

2

3

4   5

6

7

8

8. "Curbed Chair"
This piece is a nondeformable chair made by CNC. The inner structure is made of plastics. It is covered with extruded layer of walnut, oak and birch outside.

1. "Paper Furniture series-Paper Cabinet"

2. "Paper Furniture series-Paper Screen"
They hope that this piece will last forever, just like the huge classic monument. The technique of paper prop learnt from kindergarten is displayed quite interesting. The golden leaves pasted on the paper are vivid too.

3. "Pantheon"
The various themes are described in graphical, such as life, death (corpse) and wars linked with life and death. The "throw", belonging to the "throw" graphic of marcel design, is permitted to enter market as a brand.

4. "Wood Inlayed Furniture series-Overgrown with Roses"
The castle is encircled by bramble. The owner of the castle is the main character in the fairy tale "sleep beauty". The castle is shown on the tabletop with the inlaying technique. This technique is an advanced method in the field of furniture-making and one of their favorable expressing approaches. The bronze clumsy turtles (candle man) sit at the end of the table legs.
© Nacása & Partners Inc.

5. "Job's pribate room" at Design Tide Exhibition in Tokyo
The work is described as the private apartment in the castle on the exhibition in Cibone Aoama, Tokyo. They give the work a story. There used to be an eccentric guy living in the apartment. After this guy passed away, the apartment was reserved completely and opened to public. We can appreciate the elegance of the inside room-circled by the rope.
© Nacása & Partners Inc.

6. "Fool & Princes"
Fool and Princess. This piece is a graphic with the theme of Job & Nynke.

7. "Elements"
This piece is shaped with paper and belongs to the collection of layered furniture made of colorful plastics.

He graduated from Eindhoven University, majoring in industrial in 1990. In 1993, he established his own designing company. His unique works come from natural timber and factory discards. His works are the combination of the aesthetic feeling and practical function. The discards mainly include the disassembled wainscot from building, building materials from old hospital and houses, the fence of farm, etc. His creating principle is based on "reverse thinking". He starts with the selection of unique materials and creates individualized works which integrate aesthetic feeling and practical function by excellent design and technique.

His approach is in contrast with the modern one which features the adoption of latest technique. Materials and approach determine concepts. It's so time-consuming. Slow as he was, he creates impressive works. "CRISIS COLLECTION" was created in 2005. What can be created by using old CNCrotor (a sort of machine for woodcutting)? Just under such suspicion of other people, he finished his representative collection and pursued the essence of design. Simple materials and technique make him pay more attention to the each detail. All the materials he used are cheap. So the unpolished surface is easy to be scratched. But with time passes by, the 'expression of his works' has become much richer. That is the biggest power of his works.

Now the scope of his creation involves extensive fields. Besides furniture-designing, he also participates in the interior, of shop, kitchen and building held by NYMO-MA. He held an exhibition called 'Design Tide in Tokyo' in 2005 and personal exhibition in Milan in April, 2006. His new techniques draw the attention from the whole world.

Pursuing professional craftsmanship with simple materials and technique.

Piet Hein Eek
Born 1967 in Purmerend, Netherlands

Pieces of planks with different styles are conglutinated together.
It is a masterpiece reflecting discard aesthetics.

"Scrapwood series"

He collects factory discards and scrap wood, and then created the furniture series by the process of cutting and painting. The above layer is cut board. The layers below are stacks of boards. The low table and stool are finished separately. So they differ in the color and the texture of wood. That's where the power of his works lies in. These kinds of scrap wood series make him known to the world.

1

2

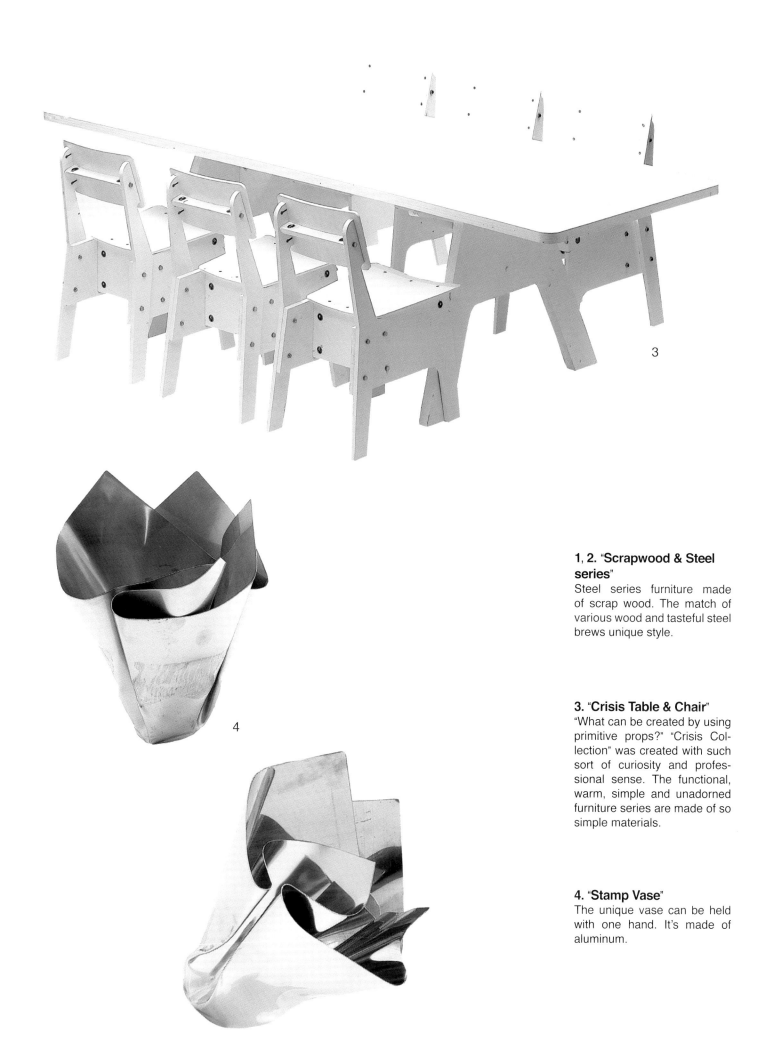

1, 2. "Scrapwood & Steel series"
Steel series furniture made of scrap wood. The match of various wood and tasteful steel brews unique style.

3. "Crisis Table & Chair"
"What can be created by using primitive props?" "Crisis Collection" was created with such sort of curiosity and professional sense. The functional, warm, simple and unadorned furniture series are made of so simple materials.

4. "Stamp Vase"
The unique vase can be held with one hand. It's made of aluminum.

Piet Hein Eek

1

2

3

4

1, 4. "Aluminum Furniture series"
The furniture series made of mineral material and Aluminum. After his processing, expressionless Aluminum is changed into unique furniture.

2, 3. "LIGHT copper & aluminum"
Extremely concise light made of copper and aluminum only. The floor light could change the position of shade.

He was born in Germany and grew up in Holland. He is one of the most distinguished designers of touch design. He was enrolled by Eindhoven University in 1996 to study design. Candle Holder and Knuckle were his initial works at Eindhoven. In addition, the well-known and unique works, such as "Hey, chair", has begun to be published and sold since then. He studied at Politecnico Milan for several months in 2000. He published two works as his graduation design at academy, namely, Burning Furniture Series and Clock Showing Time with Motion Graphics. All these works were nominated for "Rene Smeers-award" and "Melkweg-award". So he received high praise and was invited to participate in French workshop; he won the award on the design academy exhibition held in Tokyo. His smoke design has been selected onto the Moooi Collection represented by Marcel Woders, and was published on the exhibitions of Milan, London and Paris and became famous immediately. His works of smoke furniture were displayed at world art galleries such as Lidewij, Philippe and Starck. In 2004, the Gallery Moss from N.Y. held the 25th Exhibition of smoke furniture. The smoke furniture has not only impact on the burning furniture but also the works before burning furniture, such as Gaudi, Eames, Rietveld and masterpiece of Campana brothers. His works are almost one piece of furniture which belongs to the intermediate field of art, performance and design. The unprecedented innovation brought new concept to the field of design.

The innovator of touch design who created brand-new concept in the field of art, performance and design.

Maarten Baas
Born 1978 in Arnsberg, Germany

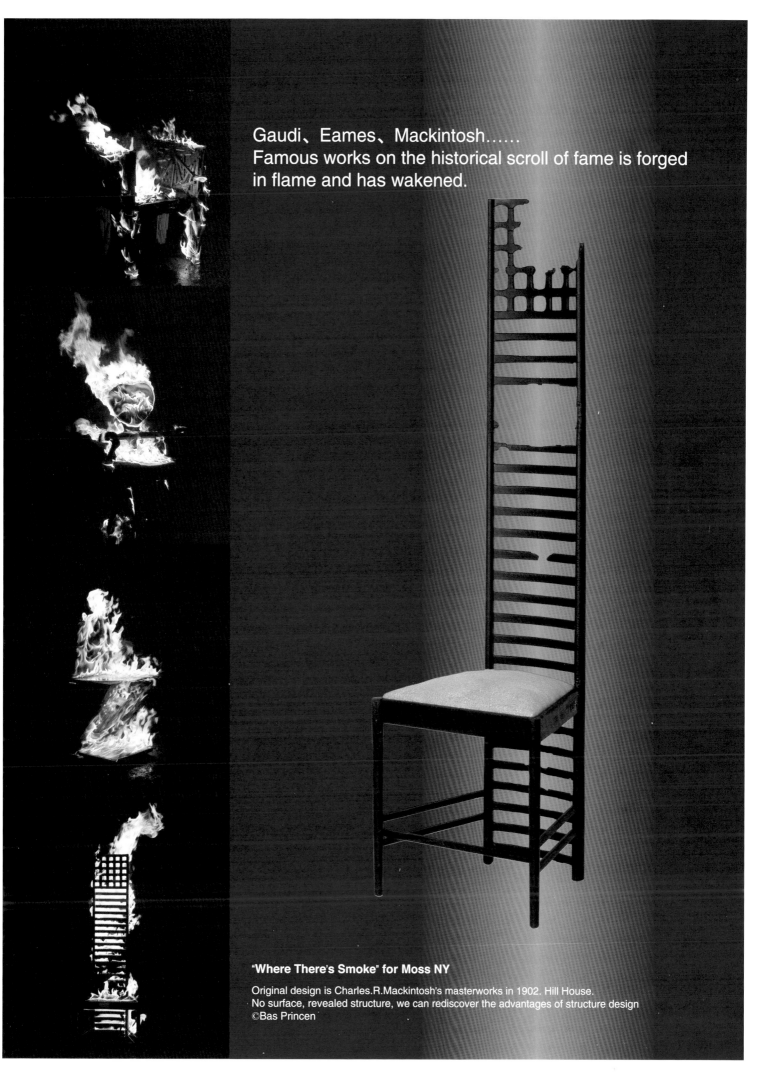

Gaudi、Eames、Mackintosh……
Famous works on the historical scroll of fame is forged
in flame and has wakened.

"Where There's Smoke" for Moss NY

Original design is Charles.R.Mackintosh's masterworks in 1902. Hill House.
No surface, revealed structure, we can rediscover the advantages of structure design
©Bas Princen

Maarten Baas

1

2

3

4

5

Maarten Baas

1

2

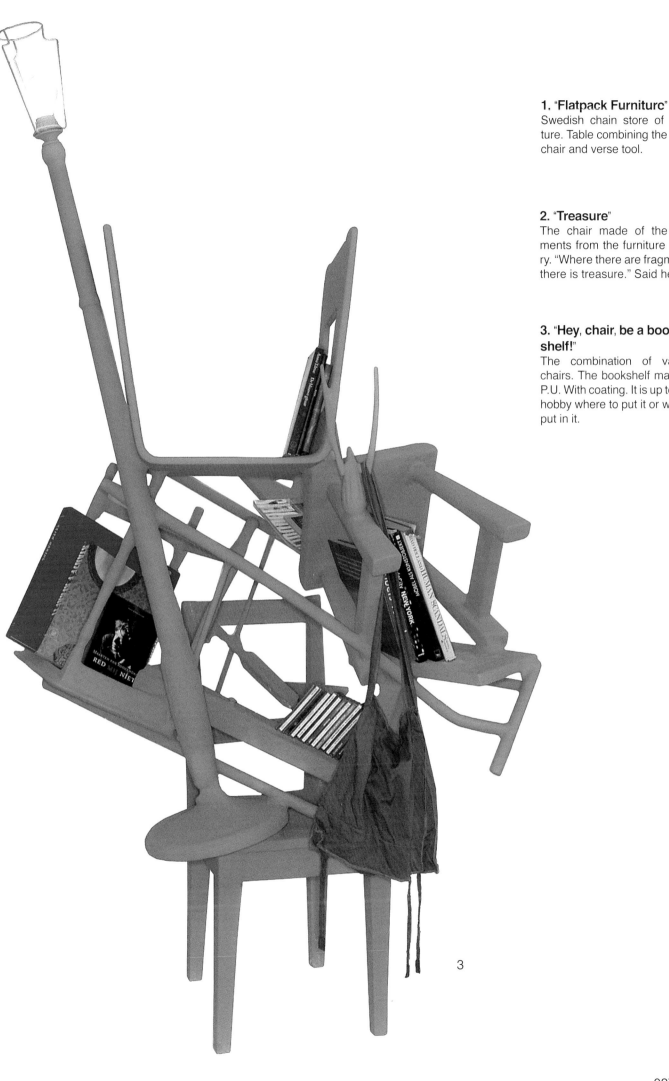

1. "Flatpack Furniture"
Swedish chain store of furniture. Table combining the IKEA chair and verse tool.

2. "Treasure"
The chair made of the fragments from the furniture factory. "Where there are fragments, there is treasure." Said he.

3. "Hey, chair, be a bookshelf!"
The combination of various chairs. The bookshelf made by P.U. With coating. It is up to your hobby where to put it or what to put in it.

3

Maarten Baas

1

07.00 AM

09.00 AM (Eppur Si Muove)

11.00 AM

2

1. "Clay Furniture"

The furniture series made of clay manually and painted with dope which can be used outside. Though twisted, there is no another one in the same form. It can only be made by hand. The designer said "just want to play with clay".

2. Shade on...

Eppurrr Si Muove ("and yet it moves"...) Galileo who published the Copernican Theory was put to trial for his deviation from the Bible. Though he admitted his mistake at the final judgment, he murmured "and yet it moves". The works from such inspiration looks abstract in form. Under the sunlight of different times, the shadow on the ground shows "EPPUR SI MUOVE".

3. "Knuckle"

The candle holder can hold four kinds of candle in size. It is early works of Eindhoven. It was made when Eindhoven was in university.

4. "Messenblok"

A knife keeper with fascinating image that inserting a knife into human's head.

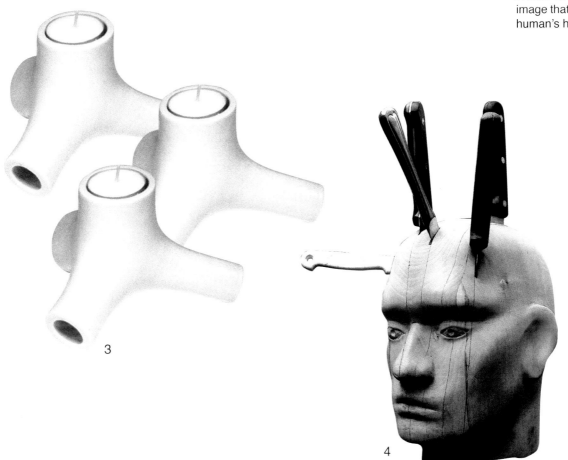

3

4

He graduated from Eindhoven Design University as a major of product design and media design. In addition, he used to study film making independently in Berlin before entering into Eindhoven. The experience then influenced his later works significantly.

He started his career when receiving the offer from Droog Design to collect his work and getting the invitation to international exhibition. He started to display his talent in the field of interior design. The main work place is Rotterdam and London. His main clients include Droog Design and Prada, O.M.A, Jurgen Bey. He provides service for client from Eindhoven city.

His design works included the thoughts of nature and suspension of human value. At the first sight, it's excellent. The message is very organic. It shows the style of a master of 21st century.

Organic design works inspire the ideal state of design for 21st century.

Simon Heijdens

Born 1978 in Breda, Netherlands

The lightening tree that appeared suddenly at the corner of the street at night.

"Tree" for city Eindhoven

In Holland nowadays, the man-made things are taking the place of the nature which is disappearing gradually, even the trees on the side of street has been laid out and managed and are no longer the natural ones. However, the designer still endeavors to make the leaves gone with the wind with the wishes that people may feel the little nature left. This works shows the trunk and leaves by the projector.
©Simon Heijdens

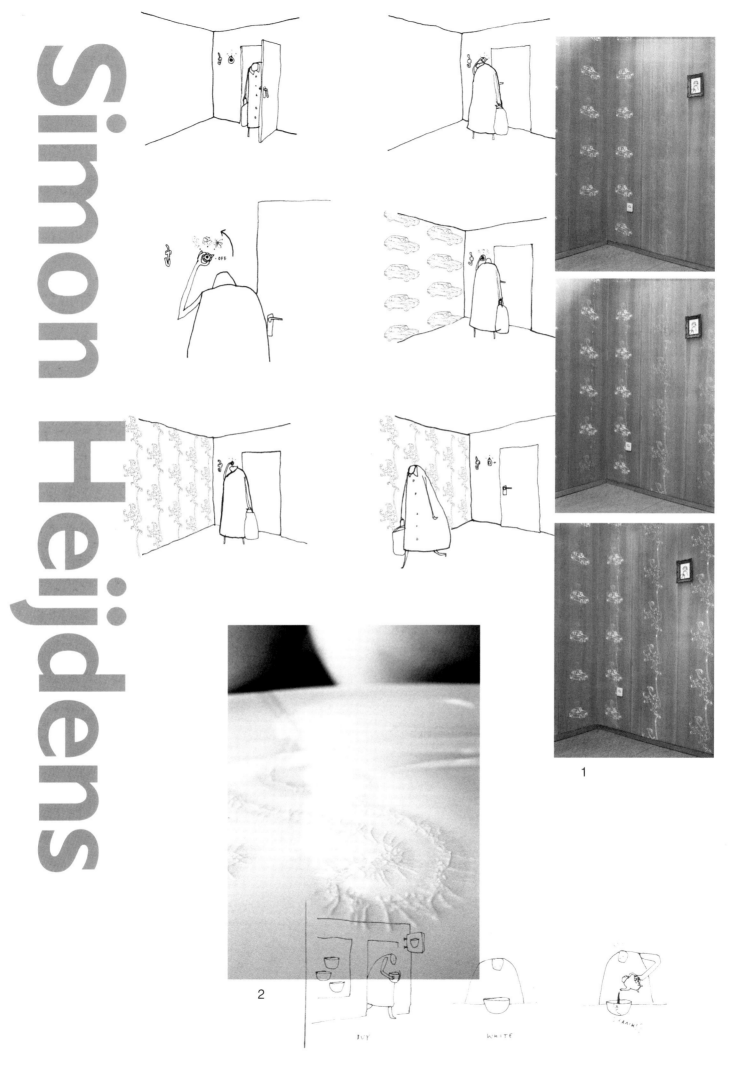

Simon Heijdens

1

2

032

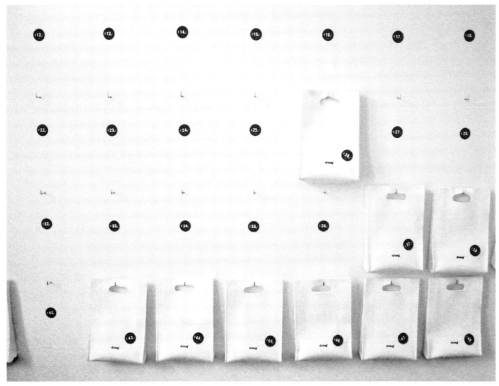

1. "Moving Wallpaper"
This piece is Eindhoven's graduation works and has become the collection of Droog design. Three kinds of patterns are shown through adding a switch.
©Simon Heijdens

2. "Broken white" for Droog design
This piece captures the splitting pattern that appears on the ceramics as the time goes by. The crackle shows the beautiful pattern of floral decoration
©Simon Heijdens

3. "50 differently priced bags" for Droog design
They are marked in price from 1 euro to 50 euro. The price of the 50 bags with same Felt is shown on the screen print. It's all up to your value of life. It became the center of focus on 2003 MILANO SALONE. It was shown in the "Your choice" Exhibition of Droog design.
©Simon Heijdens

4. "200 Sugar Cubes"
Just like the name, this piece is a set of 200 sugar cube with the number from 1 to 200 on each cube.
©Simon Heijdens

3

4

Arik Levy

He left for Europe from Israeli at the age of 27 and studied industrial design in Sweden. Now he acts on the base of Paris. After he won the designing competition in Seiko Epson, he participated in the exhibition design project in Japan. Then he returned to Europe and introduced his idea and concept of innovation. From 1992 to 1994, he taught in Ecole Nationale Superieure de Creation Industrielle (ENSCI). Then he established his own company with Pippo Lionni in the business scope of industrial design to product, package, display, interior and exhibition design. They took Europe as the center and served the international market. In addition, he participated actively in the exhibition of museum and gallery in many countries. Former clients distributed mainly in all kinds of field such as Vitra, Desalto, Ligne-Roset, Cinna, SeikoEpson, Lanvin, Bucheron, Elica, Ansorg, Renault, Baccarat, Gallery La Fayette.

They can be called as both scientist and poet. Innovation and simplicity are what he pursues in the world of art. Moreover, his complicated experience and innovative mind is the engine for his designing works.

Exploring the unique motivation of impression Interior design born in Israeli

Arik Levy

Born 1963 in Tel-Aviv, Israel

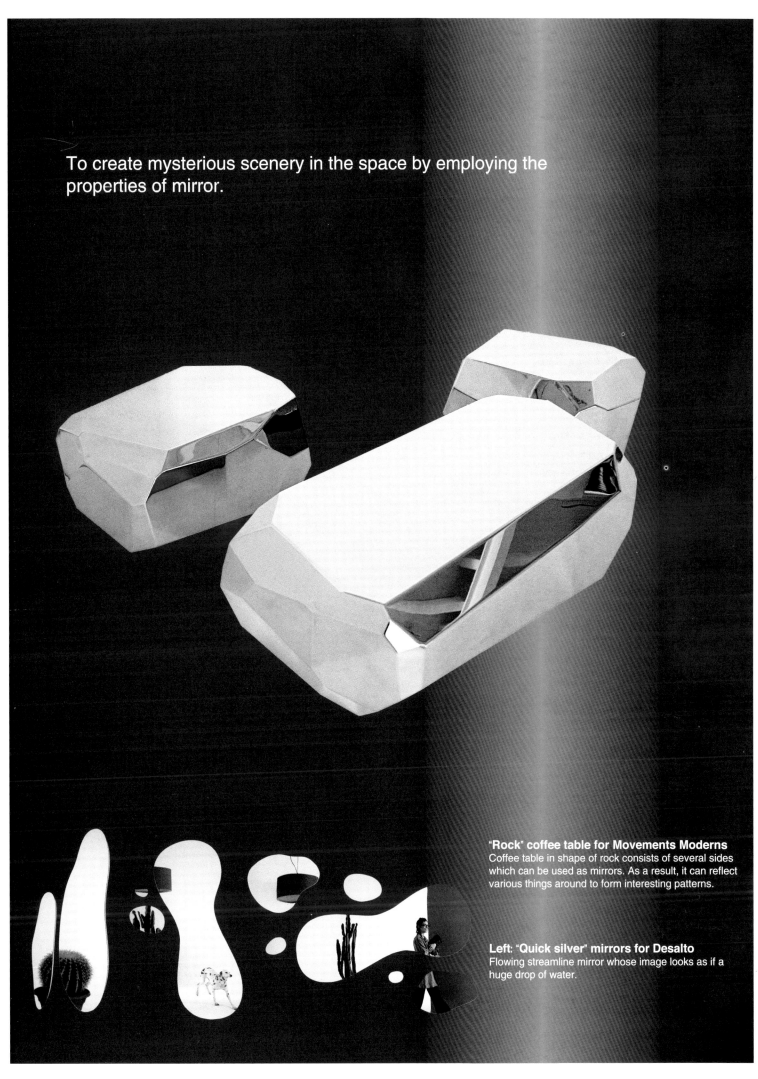

To create mysterious scenery in the space by employing the properties of mirror.

"Rock" coffee table for Movements Moderns
Coffee table in shape of rock consists of several sides which can be used as mirrors. As a result, it can reflect various things around to form interesting patterns.

Left: "Quick silver" mirrors for Desalto
Flowing streamline mirror whose image looks as if a huge drop of water.

Arik Levy

1

photo: kleinefenn@ifrance.com

2

3

1. "Umbilical" light sculptures
The light with artistic quality formed by combining shapely cable with simple bulb.

2. "Light turns"
The designer Arik controlling the light.

3. "Snob" for Gaia & Gino
Rhombic glasses concavo with big belly or concave belley.

4, 5. "Tonia & Tonia big" fruit-bowl for Ligne Roset
Fruit-bowl with flowing tuber in the middle.

6. "Galactica" fruit-bowl for Gaia & Gino
The holes take a sense of impact to people and filter the water from fruits.

4

5

6

Arik Levy

1

2

3

4

5

1. "Tina" chair for softline
Fitter chair makes your back feel comfortable.

2. "Kaz" candleholder for Gaia & Gino
The candle holder is crystal like Ice Berg. The idea is called as "nonflammable Ice Berg".

3. "Herkimer" candleholder for Gaia & Gino
Unique candleholder expresses a kind of unstable sense of asymmetry.

4. "Horizon" seating system for Baleri Italia
The beautiful sofa with the combination of straight line and curved line.

5. "Mixt" coffee table for Desalto
The coffee table is very simple. The table top in shape of ellipse shows unique expression

Arik Levy

1

2

3

4

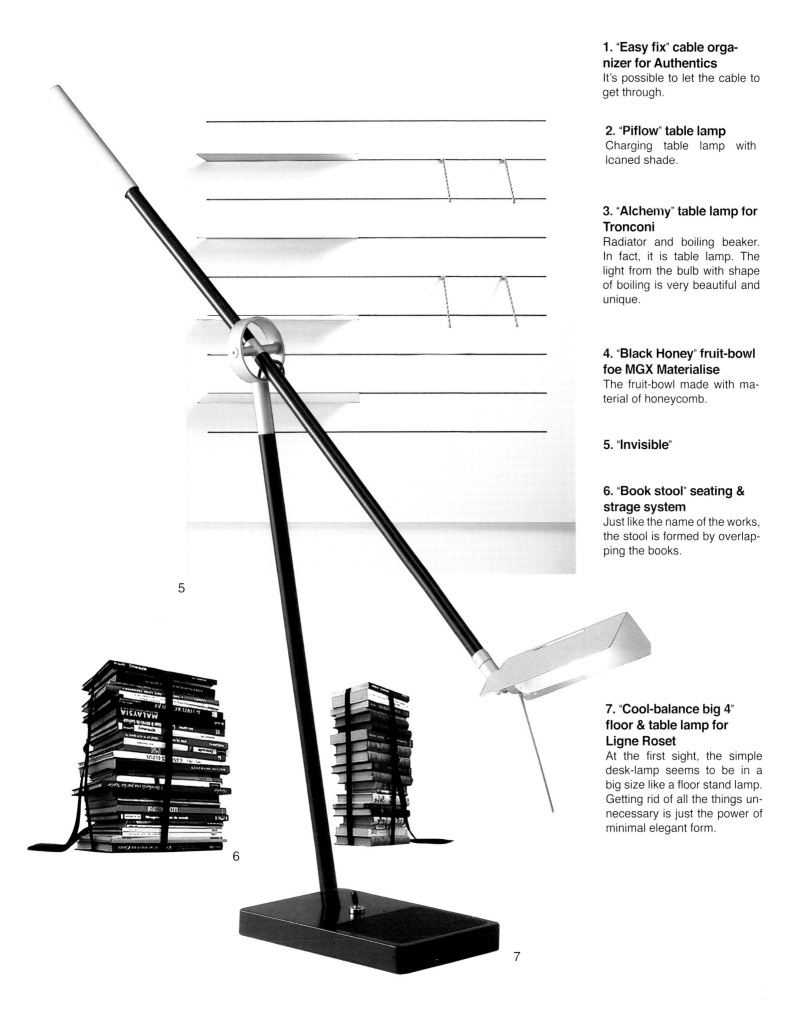

1. "Easy fix" cable organizer for Authentics
It's possible to let the cable to get through.

2. "Piflow" table lamp
Charging table lamp with lcaned shade.

3. "Alchemy" table lamp for Tronconi
Radiator and boiling beaker. In fact, it is table lamp. The light from the bulb with shape of boiling is very beautiful and unique.

4. "Black Honey" fruit-bowl foe MGX Materialise
The fruit-bowl made with material of honeycomb.

5. "Invisible"

6. "Book stool" seating & strage system
Just like the name of the works, the stool is formed by overlapping the books.

7. "Cool-balance big 4" floor & table lamp for Ligne Roset
At the first sight, the simple desk-lamp seems to be in a big size like a floor stand lamp. Getting rid of all the things unnecessary is just the power of minimal elegant form.

5

6

7

1

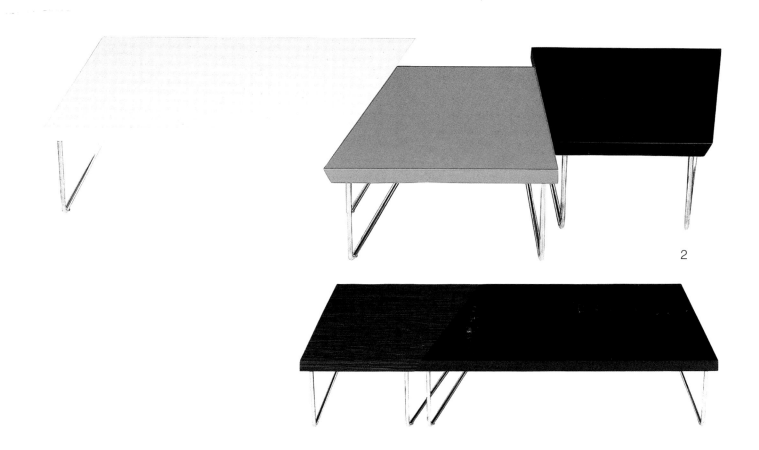

2

1. "Liko" dining & coffee table for Desalto

It is interesting that modern table-top is in contrast with plain feet.

2. "Zag" coffee table for Desalto

Tables with different sizes, color and materials. Each table can be used independently and also can be combined to quadrate table.

3. "A1" armchair for De-salto

The armchair is made according to proper angle, which let people feel commodiously and comfortable and as if embraced by the chair.

4. "Zuff" stool for Serralunga

The stool shows unique expression on the side.

5. "XL1" relax chair for Ligne Roset

The chair which people sit in for relaxing. The position of the pillow can be moved up and down.

3

4

5

Yves Béhar

He graduated from Art Center College of Design in California 1992.

He works for Lunar Design as designing leader. In addition, he used to works in frog design of Silicon Valley and was in charge of designing products from Apple Computer, Hewlett Packard and Silicon Graphics. In this period, he developed himself in the field of industrial, product, graphic packing and environment. He established his own company Fuseproject in San Francisco. This time, he created impressive and various model with discussion of new concept and attracted the attention from many people. His works covered from technology to sports, life style and fashion and attracted client with different style. The main makers were Birkenstock and Herman miller, Swarocski, MINI, Mike, TOSHIBA, Hussein Chalayan, Pacorabane, Hewlett Packard, etc.

He held personal exhibition at Museum of Modern Art in San Francisco 2004. Starting with Transformer laptop and MINI's motion strategy in 2005, his six works won gold, silver and copper respectively and got high praises worldwidely. His works has been collected permanently in Copper–Hewitt National Design Museum and SFMOMA,Munich Museum of Applied Arts, Chicago Athenaeum Museum.

From technology to fashion, multiple designs bring innovation

Yves Béhar
Born 1967 in Lausanne, Switzerland

Daily discovery starting with concern.
Science creates helpful commodities.

"Birki" for Birkenstock
These slip–on shoes can be used inside and outside the room with the aim of using as gardening outside. This is a hook on the heel. It's convenient to hang them when you don't use it.

Down: "MINI-Motion"
Watch is Mini and Festina Candino watch's corporation, carpack is Mini and Samsonite's corporation. We can read the time from watch no matter horizontally or vertically.

From 1993 to 1995, he studied construction at Chalmers University of Technology in Sweden. Then he was enrolled in Konstfac University College of Arts to study crafts and design. Later, he studied construction again in Stockholm Royal Institute of Technology from 1996 to 1999. In 2001, he established design office called Johannes Norlander Arkitektur & Forum and took Sweden as center to engage in the design for construction and furniture. In addition, he embarked on office, Johannes Norlander Arkitekur AB. As an architect and a designer of furniture, his appeal lies in that he can melt the poetic extent into the object. His works is very simple and has the features of minimal design. E&Y, Collex from Japan is his client. For both himself and Nola, "Kyparn" published in Nola can be called as master-works. A unique form is made by removing unnecessary lines. It's just like a miniature of the world.

He won Bruno Mathsson Prize in 2005 and held "Constructs" Exhibition in Stockholm in 2006.

Johannes Norlander

His philosophy is condesed and expressed by the simple and primitive design.

Johannes Norlander
Born 1974 in Gothenburg, Sweden

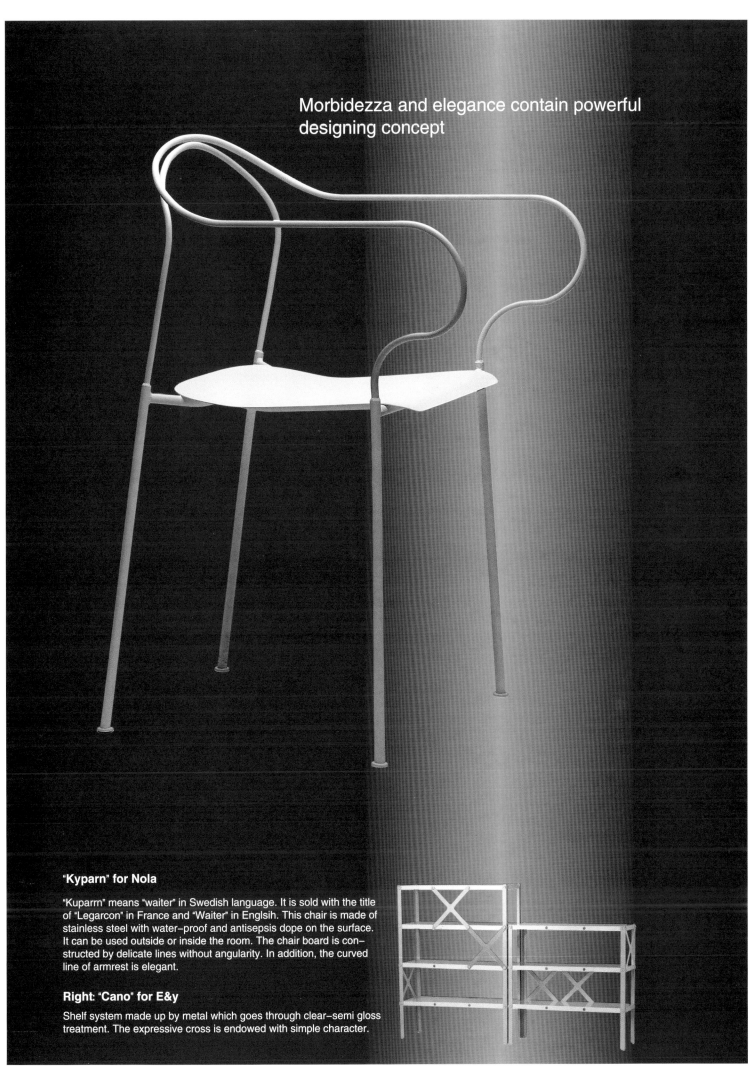

Morbidezza and elegance contain powerful designing concept

"Kyparn" for Nola

"Kuparrn" means "waiter" in Swedish language. It is sold with the title of "Legarcon" in France and "Waiter" in Englsih. This chair is made of stainless steel with water-proof and antisepsis dope on the surface. It can be used outside or inside the room. The chair board is constructed by delicate lines without angularity. In addition, the curved line of armrest is elegant.

Right: "Cano" for E&y

Shelf system made up by metal which goes through clear-semi gloss treatment. The expressive cross is endowed with simple character.

Johannes Norlander

1

2

1. Advertising design for Alcro

This is the set design made by Alcro of Sweden for its campaign. White keytone matches with gorgeous auxiliary color, which looks morc cffcctivc.

2. Office in Sweden

This is his studio in Sweden

3. "ASK" for Collex Living

Chair is firm and made of ash materials which are only available in wood. The angle of legs and the curve of arm show elegant image.

4. "A&B" for Berlinger

These are plywood with the thickness of 69mm used in assembly house system. The humdrum prefab house looks more like object after his design.

3

4

He graduated from Lcs Ateliers, Ecole Nationale Supérieure de Création Industrielle
in 1990. He immigrated into Hong Kong and
worked there temporarily. After returning to
Paris, he engaged in urban planning with Marc
Berthier, which aroused his passion to apply
design to construction. He was dedicated to all
kinds of fields from industrial products to furniture. Human is the theme of his approaches
which focuses on the research of essence. His
works are dominated by feelings, mysterious
power and realistic quality from the study on
lives. His client are distributed from Yamaha
Offshore to Renault, PoltronaFrau, Cappellini,
Cassina, Armani, Baccarat and his collection
which earned a high reputation are exhibited in
the design museum of Amsterdam, Chicago,
London, Lisbon, Paris, Zurich, etc. In 2000,
he established studio with Daniel Pouzet and
extend his design scope to the field of construction.
On the exhibition with the theme of "Human
Nature" held by Time & Style in Tokyo Design
Tide 2005, he created the coexistence of human and the nature through construction, design and project. For the product design, he
pointed out the direction of construction and
design by following the Japanese track of new
match and activity. Pondering over the forgot-
ten relationship between human and the nature was his philosophy of innovation.

The humanist in the field of interior design
Delving into the essence of human through the works

Jean-Marie Massaud
Born 1966 in France

Appealing for the coexistence of human and the nature

"STUDIO MASSAUD"
This stadium, which used to Volcano Stadium, is in commemoration of the 100 anniversary of Mexican soccer team Chivas and will be opened to public in 2006 as predicted. The approach focusing on individuality and environment links happiness, magic and vigor. He takes the whole Stadium as the symbol of life.

Left: "LIFE REEF" in Mexico
This is a housing tower located in Mexico. It is not only a housing tower, but also a vigorous space concept. Sensual is under the protection of the virtual volume. Every room and terrace is full of sense of satisfaction and safety.

Right: "MANED CLOUD"
The sky cruiser is made by taking a perspective from sky. From sky, we look at the earth. The sky cruiser holds 40 passengers and a crew of 15. It costs eight hour and forty–five minutes form Paris to Roman, four days from Paris to Madagascar. There are restaurant, lounge, library and fitness on the 500 m2 of fast deck. On the second deck with an area of 600 m2, there are 600 rooms as well as terrace, spa and bar. The size of the cruiser is L210m × W82m × H52m. The speed is 130km/h and the highest one is 170km/h.

1

2

3

4

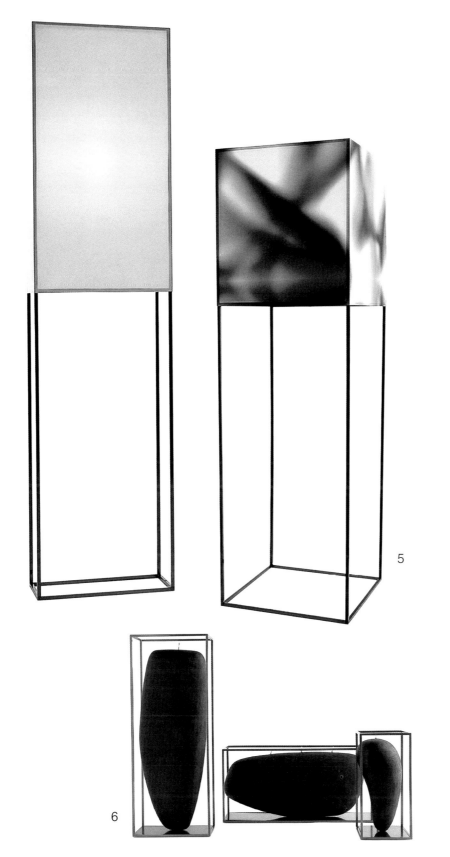

1. "Vent Blanc" for Tine & Style
This is figuline table set on the exhibition held by Time & Style in Design Tide Tokyo.

2. "NEMO" for Cacharel
This is designed for male perfume bottle of cacharel. As the universal symbol, it adopts the container in shape of frasco.

3. "ASPEN & AUCKLAND" for Cassina
He personally participated in the design of the sofa and armchair.

4. "Kennedee & Kennedee D" for Poltrona Frau
This is modular type sofa which is characterized by dynamic quality and thick line. The lightweight, portable and fashionable quilting seat and sofa are melt with traditional technique of Poltrona Frau.

5. "Cubik" for B&B Italia
This floor lamp is a trinity of clear outline, elegant shape and fabric detail, which show remarkable aesthetic sensibility.

6. "Overscale candles" for B&B Italia
These candles are designed according to construction principle in his mind. The combination of curved candles and straight frame presents strongly impact.

7. "Outline" for Cappellini
This sofa is full of line of beauty. The embrasing design let the sofa can be used as bed for rest.

©Philippe Chancel

Her father is Persian and mother is mixed-blood of Egyptian and English. She was born in Iran and then rushed about in Cambridge, Massachusetts, Germany, New York, Paris and South Africa. She studied construction at Ecole des Beaux Arts in Paris from 1980 to 1986 and then pursued her study of design at Parsons School of Desig and Cooper Union. She returned to Paris after graduation. As a art director, she jonted the design studio of Christian Liaigre and worksed there for 7 years. In 1999, she established her own studio with the name of "imh interiors". Taking Paris as the base, she is engaged in the field of construction and interior design currently.

What she values is variety. All kinds of client, project and location can arouse continuous creative inspiration. Current project is conducting in Paris, London, New York and Miami, etc. Her main works are Condesa df hotel in Mexiao City, On Rivington inNew York, Townhouse hotel in Miami , restrantDragon-I in Hong Kong , APT lounge in New York, concept of Givenchy clothing shop in Paris, Trussardi concept in Milan, etc.

She works on the base of rich imagination; the space she designs is ver elegant and changeful as if it is telling us about the essentioal story of the location. She won the designer of the year of the Maison Objet in 2004 and great hotel bathroom design award of IDEO BAIN in 2006.

The varity from the colorful experience over the world bring her resourceful imagination.

India Mahdavi
Born in Iran

The space in which the whole street
can be heard.

"Condesa df" in Mexico City
This is an inn in Mexico City. She has personally participated in the construc-
tion of concept, interior, design of furniture and collaboration of Javier Sanchez.
Responding to the warm street, such natural material as terracotta made from
natural wood is used in the interior, which adds the atmosphere of resort.
©Undine Prohl

India Mahdavi

1

1. "On Rivington" in N.Y

This is a hotel in New York. She designed and decorated for 90 rooms in person. The bathroom embedded with delicate tile shows the round mirror obviously and elegantly. To remain the atmosphere, the bedroom is also equipped with simple furniture.
©Derek Hudson

2. "Townhouse" in Florida

She personally designed the concept, the interior of 80 rooms and the furniture on the beach in Miami. In order to receive the sunshine fully from outside, the furniture in the room adopted the coordinate of white.
©Todd McPhail

3. "Apt" in N.Y

This is a pub in Meatpacking district of Manhattan. She is in charge of the concept, interior and design of furniture in lounge. Massive furniture and decoration of are deco fashion created distinguished feelings.
©Pierre Paradis

2

3

Eric Gizard

He graduated from Duperré School for Applied Arts in 1984. After working for theMichel Boyer (an architect association), UNIFA (National Union of French Furniture Industries) and VIA(Valorization of Innovation in Furnishing), he joined Nellu Rodi of fashion tride agency. He used to be a freelance. Then he established EGA (Eric Gizard and Associates) AGENCY in Paris. As a fashion group, EGA consists of ten versatile employees and is engaged in the fields of space design, such as interior design and construction. As the creator who can predicate the future, Eric won the title of designer of the year with Adrien Gardre on the maison & object in Paris in 2005.

The space and objet designed by Eric is very innovative and have strong personal quality. His inspiration is derived from the contemporary decorative art. His design is characterized by the match of light and dark from the strong contrast and special material color as well as the rational combination of tradition and modern.He has extensive interests and favorable qualities. He can participate in all kinds of projects because of his fame over the world. He has participated in design of mansion in Japan, boutique of Jean Patou in Paris, jewelry shop in Miami, apartment of London • Notting Hill and lounge of air France.

He developed the initial eclecticism into simple creation and elegant form. Flowing and smooth style is shown in the furniture of maker Aetelano, Hermes's coffecup and crystal maker Saint Louis under the lamp.

To integrate the tradition and modern with perfect innovation and create elegant style.

Eric Gizard
Born 1960 in France

Masterpiece of modernity furniture combines
simplicity and elegance

"Chauffeuse" for Perimeter
"TableBasse" for Perimeter

The emboss processing on the leather is part of Permeter Edition's collection
The elegant combination of gorgeous leather and bed foot in shape of razor.

Eric Gizard

1

1. AIR FRANCE Lounge
The new construction concept designed for the VIP lounge of de Gaulle airport in Paris. The combination of natural material oak and aluminium creates steady and elegant atmosphere.

2. House in Notting Hill
He personally participated in the design, restoration and decoration of the private house of Notting Hill in London. Reputedly, the master of the house is the couple of contemporary art collector. The works of artist David Tremlett is painted on the ceiling of dinning room.

ENSCI–LES ATELIERS graduated in 1991. The next year, he established RADI DESIGN–ERS with Olivier Sidet, Robert Stadier, Flor–ence Stadier and Cloudio Colucci who was in Japan. Cloudio Colucci used to be Idée's in–house–designer and famous in Japan. This member personally participated in the design of the Marlboro, Air France, Issey Miyake, Ricard, etc and industrial design and space design. He published the unachieved idea of product design which attracted attentions by collection and exhibition. The collabora–tion made the industrial project possible. For instance, the kitchen apparatus designed for SEB Group are the representatives.

Laurent joined RADI from 2000 to teach design and began his independent design research. He dealt with prototype projects in all the fields. Around France, he held exhibition as a cura–tor. From 2001, as the workshop director of "Domesticated Experimentations", he began teaching in ENSCI–LES ATELIERS.

From project design to exhibition curator, all showed his multi–talent.

Laurent Massaloux
Born 1968 in Limoges, France

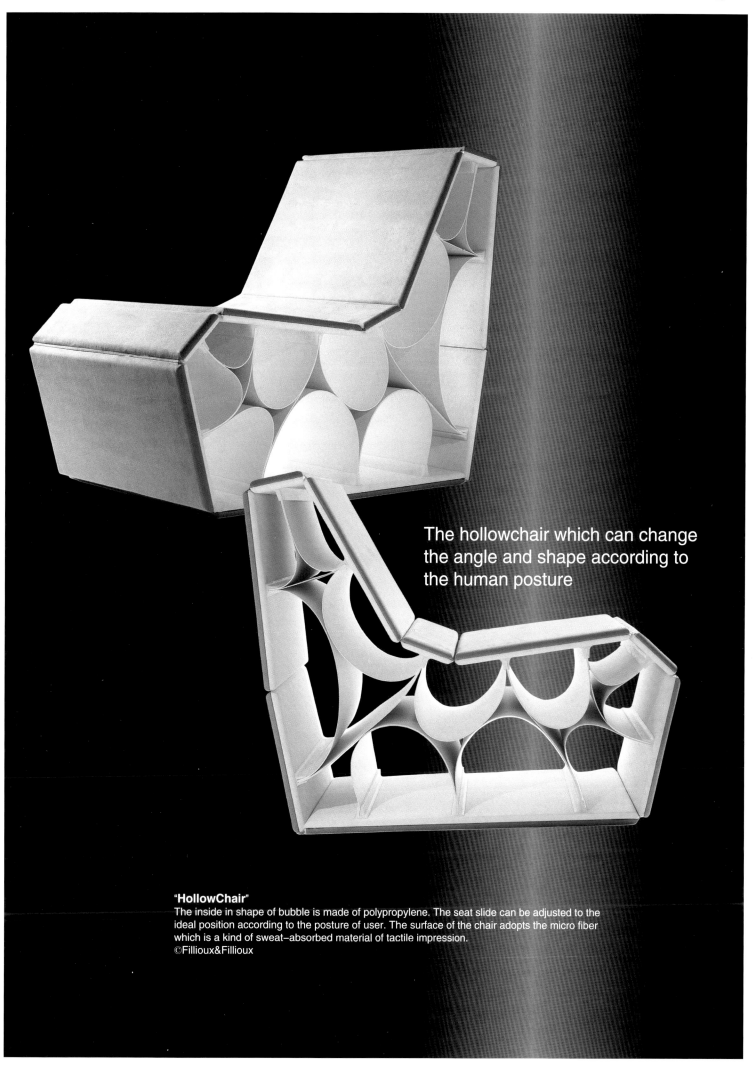

The hollowchair which can change the angle and shape according to the human posture

"HollowChair"
The inside in shape of bubble is made of polypropylene. The seat slide can be adjusted to the ideal position according to the posture of user. The surface of the chair adopts the micro fiber which is a kind of sweat−absorbed material of tactile impression.
©Fillioux&Fillioux

urent Massaloux

1

2

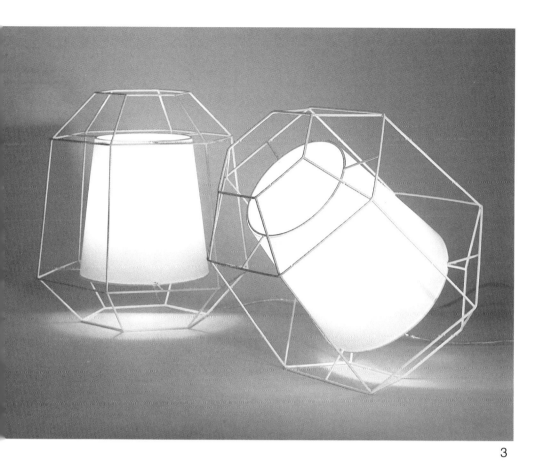

1. "Split" for EURO-RSTG BETG

This works is designed by Laurent Massalous & Olivier Sidet. The main body of the works is painted with polyurethane and the seating system of cover ring is mounted on the top. The works provides with various sitting pattern such as stool type and sofa type. Furthermore, the combination of several units can be used as mattress. As shown in the picture, many units are arranged together to form a scene of pleats.
©Oliver Sidet

2. "Audiolab3"

An integrated audio labo consists of two chairs in shape of swing, table, screen, DVD player and 8 speakers. The module is just for music and musical environment. It belongs to the collection of Luxemburg gallery, MUDAM.
©Laurent Massaloux

3. "Exo Light"

Lamp has a metal form with fluorescence paint and skeleton shade made of polycarbonate materials. The works features polyhedral structure.
©Laurent Massaloux

4. "Patere"

5. "Dessous de plat"

6. "Tabouret"

The "Vallauris" series made from ceramics and silicon is one of the projects of Laurent Massaloux/RADI DESIGNERS. The picture shows the coat hook, stool, plate and pan underlay.
©Morgane Le Gall

3

4

5

6

He studied design at University of Eindhoven. During his internship, he worked for rank Tj–epkema studio in Amsterdam. Besides design, he also studied marketing and graduated in 2003. He was famous for his graduation design "Heatwave" which attracted attention of media and is one of the collection of Droog Design,

In 2004, he established the Joris Laarman Laboratory. Now he works for the famous in–ternational institute and gallery. His main client includes Flos, Artcenica, Droog Design, DSM, Swarovski, Arco, Nissan, Domus magazine, AAlondon, Design academy Eindhoven, Fab–rica, German design Council, Stedelijk Muse–um Het Kruithuis, etc. At a young man with 27 years old, he was active on the 2006 Interna–tional Furniture Exhibition and Ideal House, etc. Moreover, he gave lesson at Fabrica Attese Ceramics Biennale.

Young Dutch desigher who entered into the world of interior scene with "Heatwave"

Joris Laarman

Born 1979 in Borculo, Netherlands

The radiator has been transformed into an artistic radiator with art nouveau style.

"Heatwave"
The works draws great attention from media. He gives life to the heater through geometric form. It is made of reinforced glass fiber. This radiator is made in module type. So the radiator can be fixed together. The minimum unit is four (specification55 × 70cm). it was collected by Droogdesign.
©Mathieu van Ek

He had studied at Delft University of Technology for 2 years and graduated from Design Academy Eindhoven. He received his master degree at Sandberg Instituut Amsterdam. Now, he carries out activities around Amsterdam. His product and furniture design belongs to the collection of Droog Design. He is the client of Philips, British, Airways, Ben, Droog Design, Levis and Heineken.

Among all the projects, his works are the perfect combination of innovative concept and visual esthetics. His works are favored by the influential clients such as KesselKramer. In 2000, he worked for Philips Design as consultant.

He was nominated for the Rotterdam Design Awards twice in 2001 and 2003. He taught at Design Academy Eindhoven and Rirtvelt Akademie Amsterdam and wrote column on the magazine of Vormberichten. From 2001 to 2004, he worked for Rirtvelt Akademie Amsterdam as the representative of designing department and won the Dutch Design Awards of the field of interior and fascio design in 2004.

Since 2002, janneke Hooymans, a female painter who had professional technique in the field of construction, design and interior design, began to participate in his works.

Visual esthetics and wisdom are transformed into elegant design of sense.

Frank Tjepkema

Born 1970 in Geneva, Netherlands

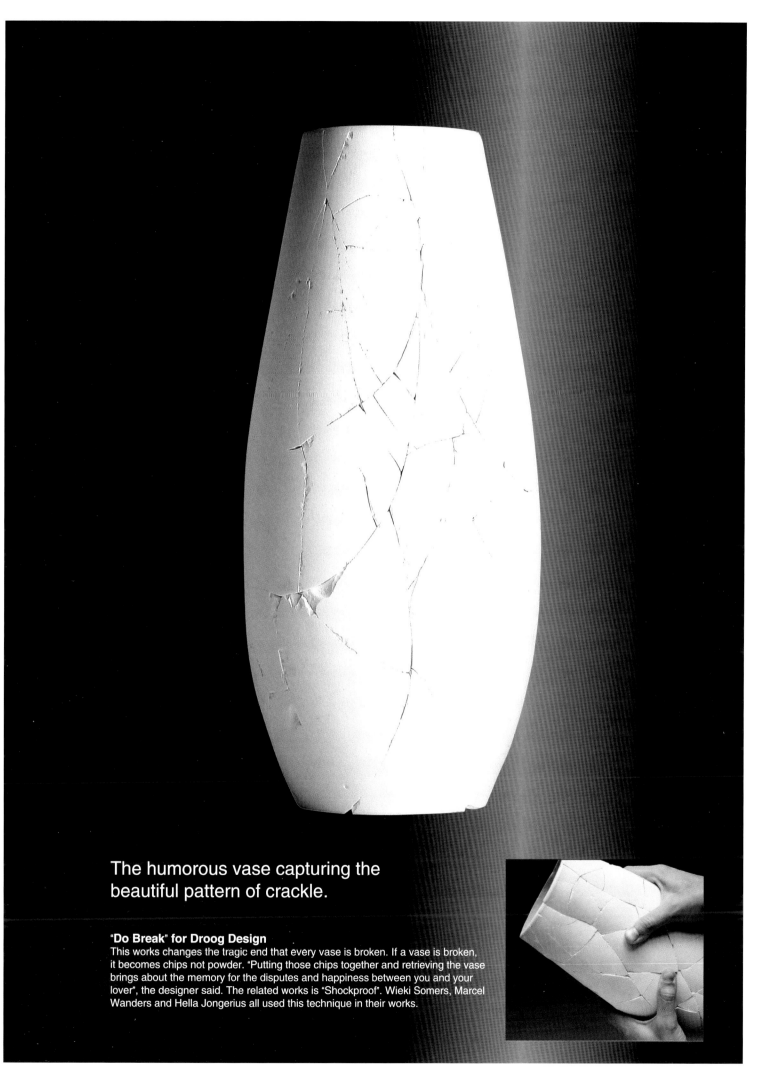

The humorous vase capturing the beautiful pattern of crackle.

"Do Break" for Droog Design

This works changes the tragic end that every vase is broken. If a vase is broken, it becomes chips not powder. "Putting those chips together and retrieving the vase brings about the memory for the disputes and happiness between you and your lover", the designer said. The related works is "Shockproof". Wieki Somers, Marcel Wanders and Hella Jongerius all used this technique in their works.

073

Frank Tjepkema

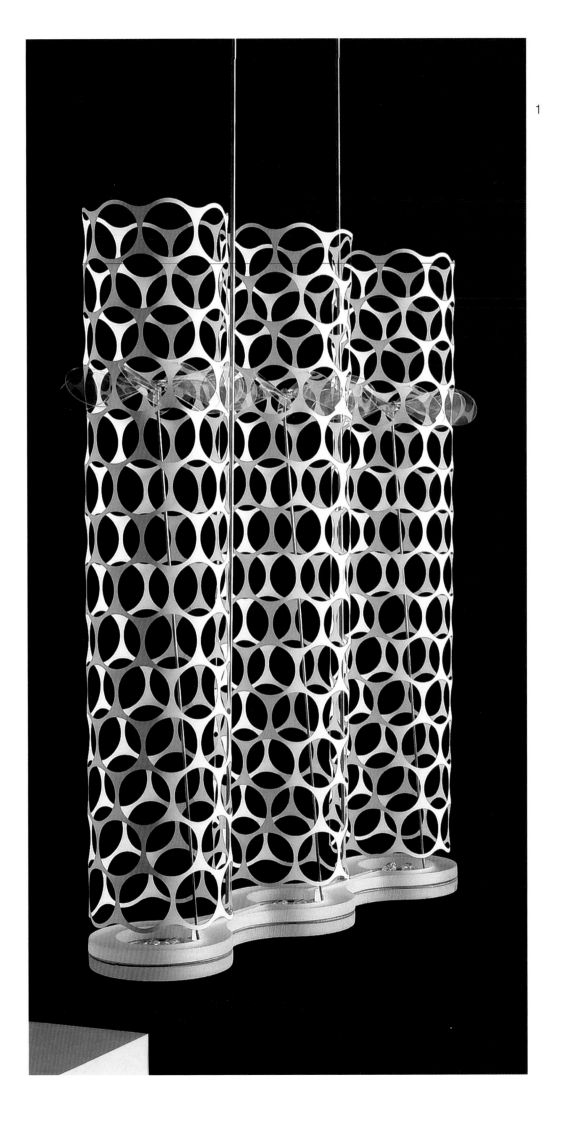

2

1. Dancing shades

The energy produced from the halogenlight operates the propeller in the shade. The movement likes the reflection of water and hypnotism with relaxing effect. It is published on the Salone Satellite in Milan in 2004.

2. "Destructive deco" for Droog Design

The design imitating the lamp by separating the veneer with laser. There are three designs, one is based on the wallpaper of traditional baroque fashion, one is pattern of 1960s, the last one is the pattern of butterfly.

3. "Maxima Willem-Alexander diamond Tiara for the wedding Maxima"

The tiara made for the exhibition held by Museum Kruithuid to celebrate the marriage of royal family Maxima and Willem Alexander. To write "I love you forever" in 100 kind of forms and the silver is embedded with diamond.

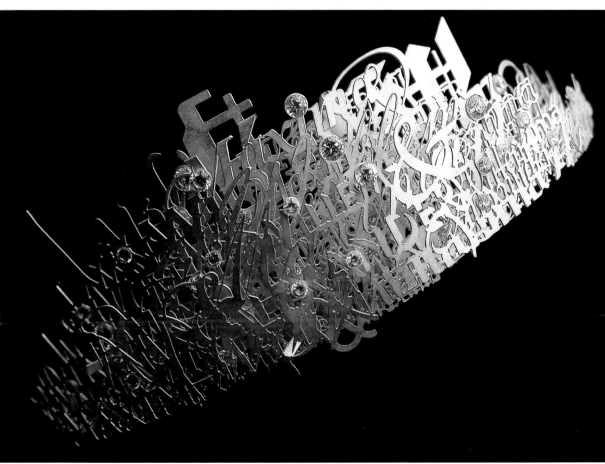

3

Frank Tjepkema

1

2

1. "Signature vases " for Droog Design

The project shows the homage to the Ron Arad and his pioneer work. The project team also includes Joris Laarman as an intern at that time. The flower base combines the choices of each member. It's made of nylon.

2. "Airco Tree" for Droog Design for British Airways

Entrusted by British Airways it's made by Droog Design for first class executive lounge of Heathrow airport in the British Airways. The picture shows the meeting place. The tree-shaped spiral structure facilitates the supply of fresh air. In 2004, it won Duth Design Awards.

3. "Tak"

Just like human can fly in the sky freely because of the invention of plane, this works makes an innovation and tries to bring the feelings of happiness and relaxation to people by the nest. This is a big sofa and consists of 50 soft gom in shape of branch, so it can expand as the growth of the family. This works is published on the Salone Satellite in 2004.

3

He designed since 1982. He created a works
with the theme of "further creation of the relationship of the human and nature" by using
the paint which had a history of 400 years.
His art crafts were very stylish, modern and
decorative and absorbed the quality of art
piece. His works is characterized by unique
quality with tradition.
Currently, he worked for original brand as
"koichiro kimura" and "art craft japan". His
tag is that it is not interesting without avant-
grade which received high praise from the pioneers of the western countries. He received
lots of offers from Colette, Saint, Printemps
in France, B&B Italia, Corso • Como in Italy,
Harrods in the U.K., MoMa (the New York
Museum of Modern Art) and Donna Karan.
After joining the Milano Salone, he went to
Dubai for development. He won many designing awards in Japan and became one of
the famous artists.

To appeal the world on the base of Japanese traditional art.

Koichiro Kimura

Born 1963 in Sendai, Japan

Tableware melting crystal and paint releases cool aesthetic feeling.

"CRYSTAL"
Series of interior spice consists of coolness, elegance and crystal. There is a set of cup, saucer and spoon. The spoon is in the front, "CRYSTAL CUP115" melting crystal and wineglass is on the left, the jewelry box, "GLOBE CRYSTAL", melting the crystal and paint is on the right. It can be used as tableware to hold Caviar.
©Shin Fujimaki / che Inc.

Koichiro Kimura

1

2

3

4

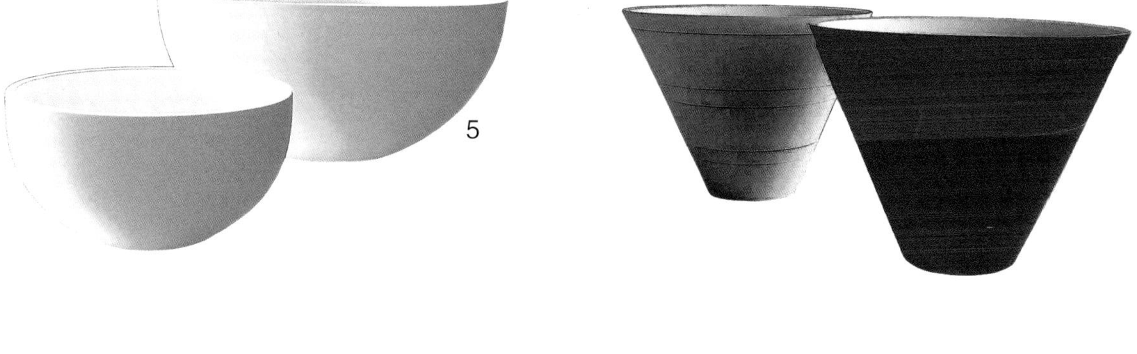

5

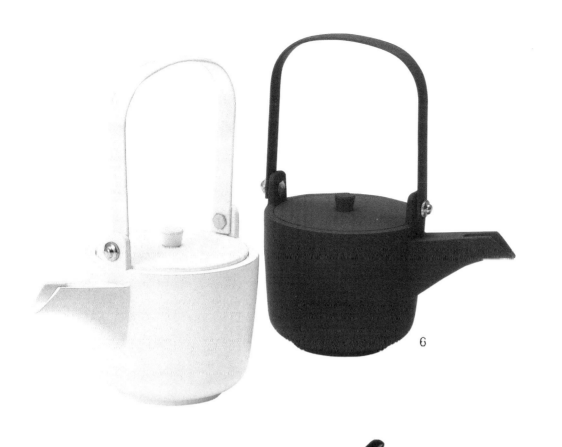

1. "NEW WAVE"
The cup and saucer in gilt fashion.

2. "GOLD"
Bowl set in gilt fashion
©Shin Fujimaki/che Inc.

3. "GOLD"
Round palte set and globe with series No.2
©Shin Fujimaki/che Inc.

4. "PHARAOH, FOR YOUR LOVE"
One of his favorite works, PHARAOH. The box forming the shape of Pyramid

5. "BOWLS", "ENSUI"
The bowl with the effect of fluorescence is novel and twinkling.

6. "CHOSHI"
Flagon with tactile impression of Mat and steady impression.

7.8. "NEW WAVE"
The series of WAVE are characterized by elegant curves and bright combination of color.

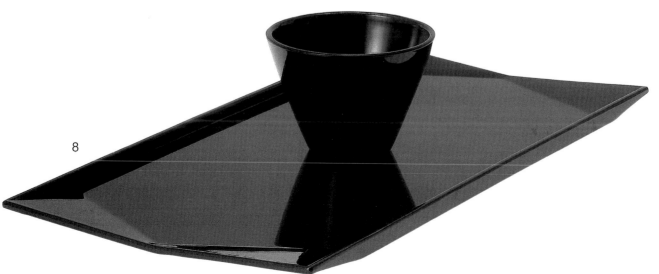

Ineke Hans

From 1986 to 1991, he studied 3Ddesign at Hogeschool voor de Kunsten Arnhem and got mater degree of furniture design at Royal College of Art Londun in 1995. The passion for carving and the industrial experience confirmed her designing career. After working in Britain for 3 years, she established her own studio with the name of INENE HANS/ARNHEM in Olanda. She personally participated in the design of furniture and other products from event to interior. She also was engaged in the design of her own collection and published in the world.

At beginning, her works focused on people's imagination and behavior on the base of the belief of the mysterious power from the product and environment. "The recognition of the relationship between human and things is the premise of design." Said she. Some of her works showed the essential image and national tradition by using the color and form.

Using natural form and bright color to express the essential national tradition

Ineke Hans

Born 1966 in Netherlands

The furniture which creates warmth,
taking the nature as the core.

"JOLLY JUBILEE" for Arco
Lovely chair with the height of 70cm
Material is MDF. The surface is roof pattern by pressing.

1

2

3

Ineke Hans

1. "Black Magic-laser chair"
The material is MDF cut by laser. Using modern and traditional technique, concept on the base of handmade style, pattern expressed by laser, the simplicity suffused everywhere.

2. "Ordinary Furniture-relax set"
Low- position table & chair set with the table and chair height of 30cm. This is designed to remove the default and inconvenience of the former furniture. It is made of recycled plastics and can be used inside and outside. For the size, it is suitable for public space.

3 "FOREST FOR THE TREE" for Lensvelt
The coat stand with the height of 180cm. The cut metal materials are colored by laser cover with red, black, brown3, etc.

4. "Black Beauties-happy horse"
Cockhorse for Babies is used for celebrating friends' marriage and bearing. Because of the recycle plastics, it can be used in the bathroom and outside the room.

5. "Black Gold-modular porcelain"
Black porcelain coffee set. The modular porcelain was formed with 5 shapes and tube corner and pison in 3 sizes. As a result, the queer form appeared.

6. "GARLIC CRUSHER" for Royal VKB
The garlic crusher can avoid the touching with garlic and lighten the odd of garlic.

4

5

6

nendo

The design unit led by ・OOKISATOU consists
of 6 mumbers such as Takayuki Ishikawa, Aki-
hiro Ito, Takahiro Matsumura, Teruaki Okada
and Yoshitaka Ito. Its representative is SATTO,
who was born in Canada 1977. He established
Nendo in Tokyo after receiving the master degree from the SILS University in 2002 "What is
Nendo?" As answered by SATTO, the unit offers
the products which are diverse and soft. Though
there is no advantage in the number of members, the unit deals with wide business such as
building design and CG/mock. The responsibility
is clear in the unit. They can adapt to the client's
needs. They have lots of clients both at home
and abroad.
They carried out diverse business around construction design, product design and CI design.
All are from cutting and carving. They combine
the joy and beauty. That's the design of nendo.
The following are the awards and main exhibitions.
In 2002, they won "compe grand prix" and "design compe" on 15th international students design competition.
In 2003, they won special award on Design Re-
port exhiblted on Salone Satellite and held exhibitions in Tokyo Design Center and Living Design Center OZONE.
In 2004, they participated in the all kinds of international furniture exhibitions in Pairs, Koln and
Stockholm. They exhibited Shanghai-hai cool
on Shanghai Sino-Japan-Korea Exhibition and
published "chab-table" for DePadova, lighting-
speaker "sorane" for Oluce and low table "snow"
for Swedese.

"Can do" with no limitation
Creative unit which creates products with free imagination

Nendo
From Japan

Snowflakes fall on the low table. It's so romantic.

"snow" for Swedese
The pieces are like snowflakes on the low table.

nendo

1

2

3

1. "Yuki" for Cappellini
The partition is like a wall formed with snowflakes.

2. "wind" for Swedese
Stool seems to swing in the wind. Minimal element and ultra-thin board deliver strength. Keeping the warmth of wooden furniture, leaving the smooth and sharp impression to people.

3. "chab-table" for DePadova
In daily life, the chab-table can be used when it is in need. The Japanese tea room is changed into the flexible space such as living room, dining room and bedroom, etc. The chab-table can be used as side table in the high position and coffee table in low position. The tray can be removed and used as bed.

4. "Home" Private house SHIKINEJIMA Tokyo
The shelf surrounds the outside to protect the privacy and makes the house like a library. The semi-transparent FRP and space between shelf boards guarantee the delivery of sunlight to rooms. At night, in the moonlight, the house seems to be unified with the moonlight. The works won the excellent prize on JCD design.

4

Chris Kabel

After graduating from Eindhoven Design Uni–versity in 2001, he acted on the base of Rot–terdam. The project of his graduation design still continues, one of it is "Sticky Lamp" which became permanent collection of Droog de–sign and displayed on the Hotel Droog of Mi–lano in April of 2004. "Sticky Lamp" not only can be used as lamp but also can be used as modular lamp like chandelier. The other one is "ADDFUNCT glass" which will be produced and sold by Mobach according to the plan. His works became a part of the collection of Stedelijk Museum in Amsterdam. Now he has lots of clients including Droog design, moooi, Heineken, Levi's, Volkswangen in the field of clothes, jewelry, furniture and drink. "Sticky Lamp" was exhibited by moooi on 2003 Mi–lano Salone and 2004 100%design. That is his representative works. The gas lamp is the combination of modern technology and glacis design. He hoped that the works could deliver the sense of authenticity.

To achieve the coexistence of authentic function and unique design ironically

Chris Kabel
Born 1975 in Haarlem, Netherlands

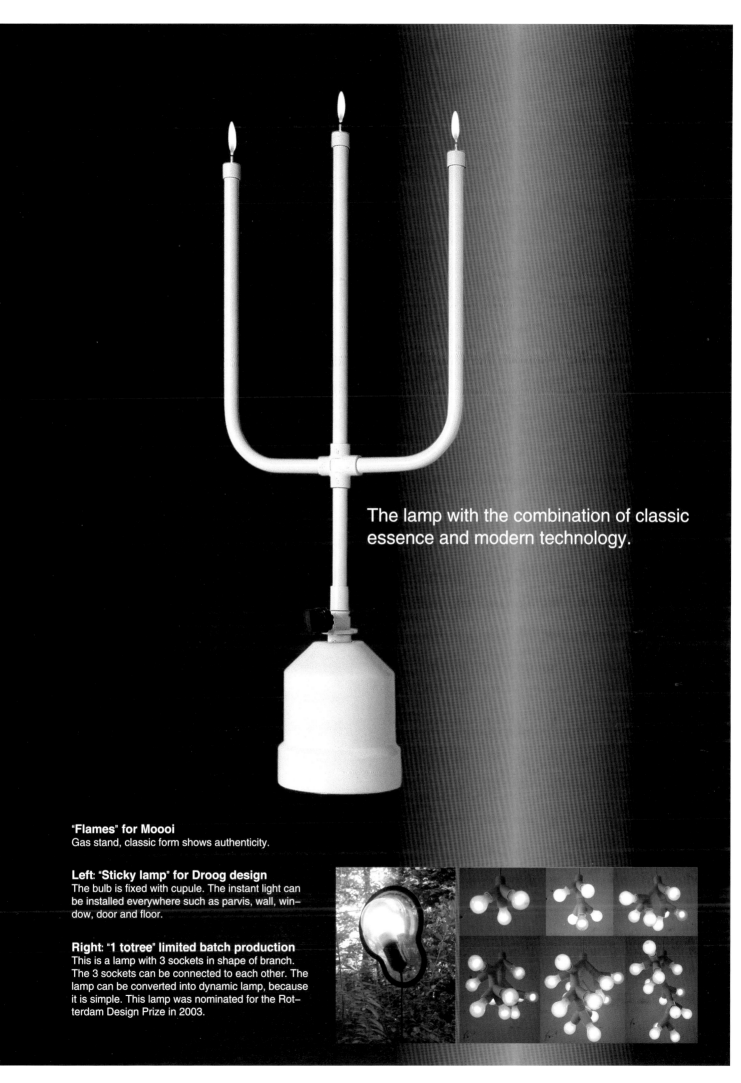

The lamp with the combination of classic essence and modern technology.

"Flames" for Moooi
Gas stand, classic form shows authenticity.

Left: "Sticky lamp" for Droog design
The bulb is fixed with cupule. The instant light can be installed everywhere such as parvis, wall, window, door and floor.

Right: "1 totree" limited batch production
This is a lamp with 3 sockets in shape of branch. The 3 sockets can be connected to each other. The lamp can be converted into dynamic lamp, because it is simple. This lamp was nominated for the Rotterdam Design Prize in 2003.

Chris Kabel

1

2

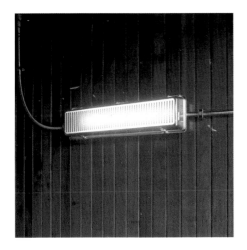
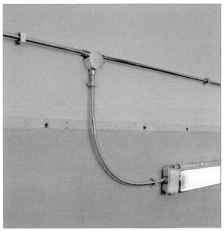

1. "Shady lace" for Droog-design
To be under the Parsol is just like to be in the shade of trees

2. "Plant tape" limited batch production
The tape is cut into the shape of leaves.

3. "Gold circuitry"
The circuitry is usually hidden in the wall. This device can be used as gold plate if installed outside.

4. "Mesh chair" for Sofa foundation
The chair is usually covered. If the cover is removed, the structure of the chair will be revealed.

3

4

Eye-catching designers of new generation

Abundant imagination would let people feel happy, feel childlike innocence and let fairy tale occur in reality… Only the works created by the desire from creation can be reserved in the visitors' mind. Their works always come into our sight unconsciously and attract our attention gradually. Few as their works, every piece express their personality and love to us. From their works, it seems that we could hear their words that design may bring happiness to people.

COMMITTEE

The unit of two designers is formed by Clare Page and Harry Richardson. They were both born in 1975. After graduated from Liver Pool University as majors of fine art, they moved to London. They got married and established COMMITTEE in 2001. Taking furniture, lighting and textile as core industry, they are engaged in the field of interior design. Their main works are as the followings: Knit Accessory for Topshop in London, "Kebab Lamps" published on Milano Salone in 2004, "Origami Desk" published on Koln Furniture Fair, etc.

"Kebab Lamps" series are their most representative works. They combined the tableware of middle ages with the waste to make a stand lamp in shape of foot. This unique design has become a mush–talk story. This works was made by Thomas Goode model who was a Royal Tableware Maker. During the Design Tide in Tokyo in 2005, they held collection exhibition of Kebab Lamps in CIBONE AOYAMA. In addition, they converted the graphic into limited edition of fashion item and conducted the production, sale and exhibition, which attracted attention from the art shop and gallery of high sense at home and abroad.

Adding art spirit into waste, creating new value

COMMITTEE
From UK

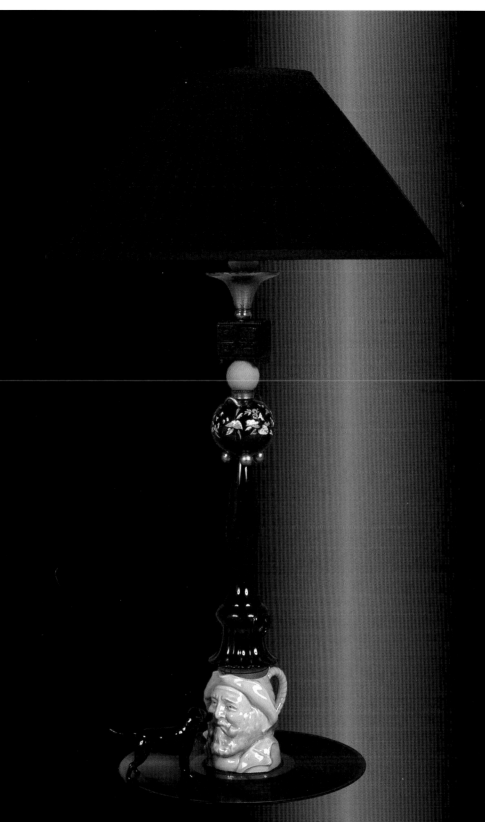

The lamp conveys the idea of changing waste into valuable

"Kebab Lump"

This works was published on the furniture fair of Milan in 2004. The materials used in this collection containing every theme are useless and thrown waste. To recognize the importance of the waste is the belief of the design.

Left: "Fly Tip" illustration

The wallpaper displayed by Design store during the Design Tide in Tokyo is characterized by the illustration that the dustbin was overturned.

After studying basic course of art design at the Art School of Prinston University in the UK, he studied graphic design at Exeter University from 1985 to 1988 in the UK. After graduation, Richard Frost, a news and advertising photographer, became his teacher. In 1991, as a photographic illustration, he began his career of freelance. From 1995 to 2005, he worked for Plymouth University as an instructor of photography department. In 2005, he became the focus on the exhibition of designersblock in London. In the same year, he held the installation of Tide Chandelie in Comme Des Garcons store (Dover St. Market) London. In 2006, he held exhibition of SCRAP ONLY in Toolsgalerie, Paris. He has many clients, such as DaimlerChrysler, Honda, Sony, BBC, Times, GQmagazine, Esquire Magazine, etc.

He is engaged in many fields, such as advertising, design, publication of books, editing of magazines, etc. Now he is busy in making several permanent illustrations. Recently, he is conducting a design project with the concept of collection. He will collect a good number of materials and assemble them together to endue them with new meanings and various configurations. For instance, to combine small articles together and assemble them into chandelier, illustration and tri-dimensional practical works. It is of significant value especially in the field of design that the waste and industrial products are applied to such expensive works as chandelier.

Taking the material-collecting as the concept and create new value from it.

Stuart Haygarth
Born in UK

The waste on the shore is converted into new valuable thing

"TIDE CHANDELLER"
There are many illegal wastes on the Kent shore in Britain and it took him about 2 years to collect the waste. He classified the wastes by transparent and translucent plastics, then changed these waste with various shape into balls which symbolize the tides in–fluencing the waste on the shore and the moon influencing the rise and fall of tides.

Right: "MILLENNIUM CHANDELIER"
This chandelier is made of 1000 crackers of PARTY POPPERS which is collected on January 1st from the celebration of MILLENNIUM in London. The shape is like a plant swing in the wind.

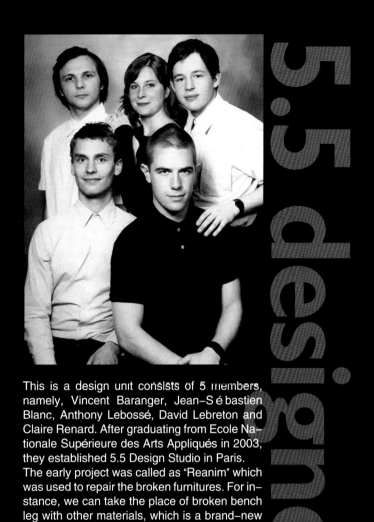

This is a design unit consists of 5 members, namely, Vincent Baranger, Jean-Sébastien Blanc, Anthony Lebossé, David Lebreton and Claire Renard. After graduating from Ecole Nationale Supérieure des Arts Appliqués in 2003, they established 5.5 Design Studio in Paris.

The early project was called as "Reanim" which was used to repair the broken furnitures. For instance, we can take the place of broken bench leg with other materials, which is a brand-new technique. This project succeeded on the exhibition of La gallerie de la Salamandre and was displayed on the furniture fair in Paris and Pitti Living held by Christina Morozzi in Italy.

His works were displayed on the exhibition of Biennal of Design of Saint Etienne in 2004 and agnès .b held by designer's block in Tokyo, and then he was entrusted by the old department and gallery Lafayette of Paris to design new shop Lafayette V.O for the young generation.

Now he collaborates with many makers, such as Salviati, Arc, Ozé, Bernardaud, Galeries Lafayette and b-ton design, to pursue the originality and practicability of design. They also participate in the workshop of art school and design school regularly. We shall wait expectantly for the development of their works combining the art and design.

New belief of design from the unique idea, design unit with expectation of France

5.5 designers
From France

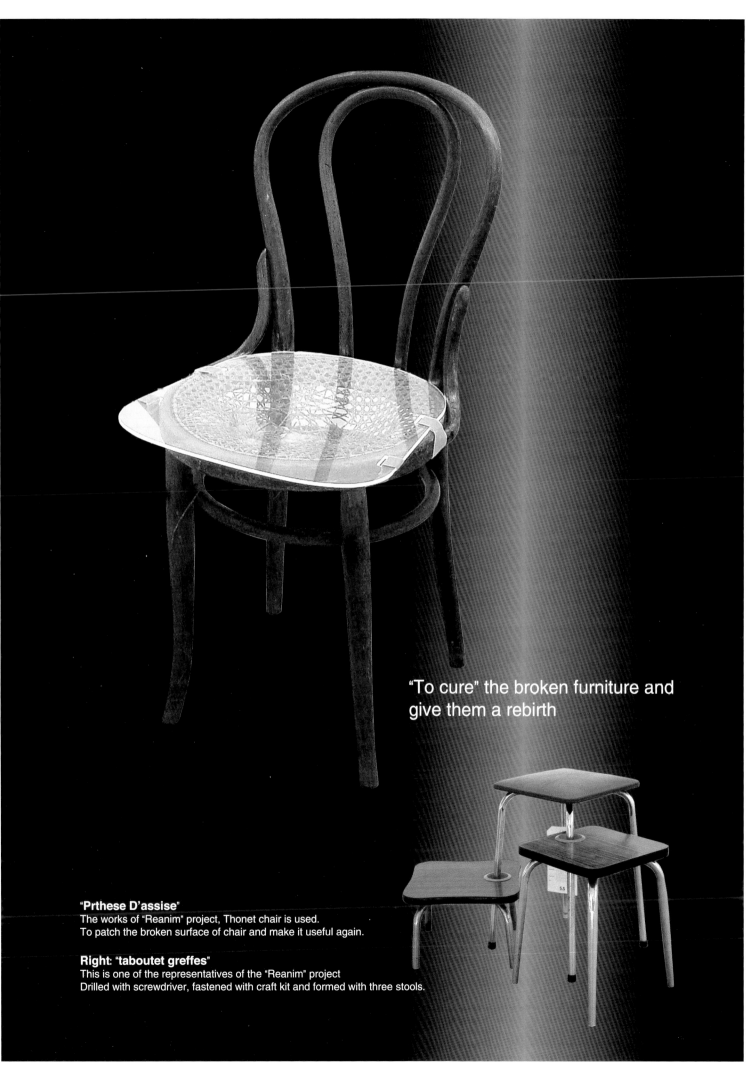

"To cure" the broken furniture and give them a rebirth

"Prthese D'assise"
The works of "Reanim" project, Thonet chair is used.
To patch the broken surface of chair and make it useful again.

Right: "taboutet greffes"
This is one of the representatives of the "Reanim" project
Drilled with screwdriver, fastened with craft kit and formed with three stools.

5.5 designers

1

2

1. "Sauclere Filage n.8" for Bernardaud
This works belongs to the project of "ouvriers-designers" which is created in cooperation with Bernardaud, a pottery maker. During this project which is one of their important projects, they participated in the Biennial, which made them more famous.

2. "Presse citron de star"
This works is one of the "ordinary objects" which is with the view to the simple things used in daily life and with the aim of rebuilding new logo. The design with 3 brackets, which can achieve our dreams and is full of imaginations, reminds us of Philippe Starck's famous "Juicy Salif" (Aless).

3. "Defects of deco"
This is one of their projects. The glass handles of the tableware like the knife, fork and spoon can be detached and changed. Such design brings uniqueness to the common tableware.

3

1

2

3

4

1. "Saladier Calibrage n.3" for Bernardaud

This works also belongs to the project of "ouvriers-designers". The salad cans of this series, form No.2 to No. 16, are various in design.

2. "Cremier Coulage n.11" for Bernardaud

This also belongs to the project of "ouvriers-designers". The patterns are printed interiorly. The inverted design is quite interesting.

3. "Tasse Garnissage n.5" for Bernardaud

This works is designed by "ouvriers-designers". Tasse is referred to the mug with handle and Garnissage is referred to interior decoration. According to what mentioned above, this works means that the handle is put in the mug.

4. "Anse de sucre" for La Corbeille

This also belongs to the project of "ouvriers-designers". The handle of cup is made of granulated sugar.

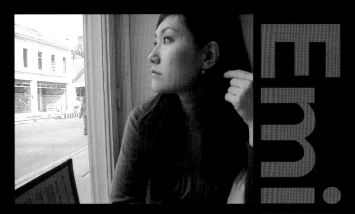

She graduated from Kingston University BA Furniture and Product Design in 2002 and Buckinghamshire Chiltern University College MA Furniture Design & Technology as president in 2004. At present, he works as a product designer in London.

Beginning with displaying her works on the exhibition of Victoria & Albert Museum Light Entertainment in April 2004 after graduating from university, she always actively participates in the exhibitions. She displayed Trophy Tableware on the Milano Satellite in April of the same year and her graduation design of MA, the design of 100% East Stand, in the Vitra commodity showroom of London in 2005. She displays his works with an architect in the Vivienne Westwood Shop on MILANO SALONE 2006.

The inspiration of representative "Trophy Tableware" is from her interest of "Cup". The cup has no use except decoration. The World Cup is an example in case and the Cup symbolizes Sports & Power which is the impression for males. So she intended to design an opposite and practical Cup symbolizing the hazy impression of females and hoped that the user could experience the different interest of dining by Trophy Tableware. That is where her designing belief lies in.

Japanese female designer who designs the dreams and impression of females

Emiko Oki
Born in Tokyo, Japan

Make the common dining more special.

"Trophy Tableware"
A set of single tableware consists of 7 wares, namely, cup, saucer, soup bowl, salad can, eggcup, teapot and dinner plate. Placed in right order, these tableware would show a shape of Cup and could serve as decoration when not used for dining. The materials are pottery with 3 colors, namely, white, black and milk-white. At present, the limited edition made of platinum and bronze is under manufacture.

Wieki Somers

After graduating from The Design Academy Eindhoven in 2000, she got down to works immediately and took Rotterdam as the base. She designed for Droog Design, Chi ha paura and held many exhibitions. Her project of "Muffins" received high praise and was nominated for Rotterdam Design Priza of Nieuwegein Young Designers Award.

Her works are characterized by the interlacement of practicality, materials, belief and sentiment. She searches repeatedly for the most important property and practicality of the materials during the selection of materials. When it comes to using glass, metal, pottery & porcelain, cloth and synthetic fiber, she will let these materials work with common natural elements, such as water, air, fire, etc. What she values most is to make out popular works. So her works express profound meanings and she put comprehensive requirement on technique, technology and shape. She is inspired from the original Dutch legend, so she is fond of traditional technique and works. The works combining common natural elements with non–natural ones may convey a kind of familiar impression, meanwhile, give the appreciator a kind of mysterious feelings. For instance, in the work of "High Tea Pot", she adds decadent pelage to the skull and adds practicality to fragile porcelain, which creates multiplex esthetic impression, meanwhile, the teapot itself may get the functional impression.

Eye–catching style conveying both wildness and poetry, the new blood of the second generation of Dutch designers

Wieki Somers

Born 1976 in Sprang–Capelle, Netherlands

The teapot with aesthetic wildness of the theme of animals

"High Tea Pot"
This wild porcelain teapot with the theme of animal. The pelage of beaver can be used to keep warm.

Wieki Sommers

1

2

3

1. "Soap Bubbles"
This is a lamp made of gray glass. She is inspired from the bubbles in the half-full shampoo bottle. A bunch of romantic bright from the frosted glass.

2. "Blossoms"
The vase integrating with the plant within it is made of glass and pottery & porcelain.

3. "Matress stone bottle"
This is a pattern of reticulation made of junction plates. The materials are pottery & porcelain. This works won the Do sign Prize Rotterdam 2003.

4. "Bathboat"
The bathtub in shape of boat is floating on the surface of water just like item 6.
©Elian Somers

5. "Muffin"
A lovely stool with height of 40cm. The materials are synthetic resin. This works was nominated for Design Prize Rotterdam2001 and won Marerial Prize2003.

6. "Bathboat"
The bathtub made of ceramic materials with the weight of 200kg. The designing belief is to let it float and swing on the water surface.

4

5

6

111

She graduated from Rietveid Academie Amsterdam in 2003 and has studied the techniques of glass, textile and silver–smelting in college. With the interest in organism, she is studying taxidermy at present.

Her works is the combination of glass, silver textile and specimens. Embroidery on the ear and ear–rings with embedded silver convey her aesthetic consciousness of individuality.

This works is named "Fantasy vs Reality". What will happen if the fantasy is actualized? How to compare the reality with the fantasy? Furthermore, the reality is expressed by fantasy. Based on these subjects, she employed the specimens of animals which are used to express the character or the character in the fairy tale and legend.

In 2001, she won the Genomineerd Dutch Design Award, and then began to participate in exhibition. In 2004, she held personal exhibition in Paris and London. During the MILANO SALONE in 2005, she held exhibition in Anytimesoon.nl Galerie of Milan. Nowadays, the decoration in taxidermy studio become popular unconsciously and her queer design catches more and more attention.

Taxidermy magician who relives the horrible but gorgeous animals.

Afke Golsteijn
Born 1975 in Amsterdam, Netherlands

Taxidermy art concealing the brutality,
flesh and beauty

"Ophelia"
The title of the work comes from Ophelia, Hamlet's lover, in the
tragedy by Shakespeare. The designer was inspired from the
fact that Ophelia usually wears lots of gold ornaments and this
works is ironical.

Afke Golsteijn

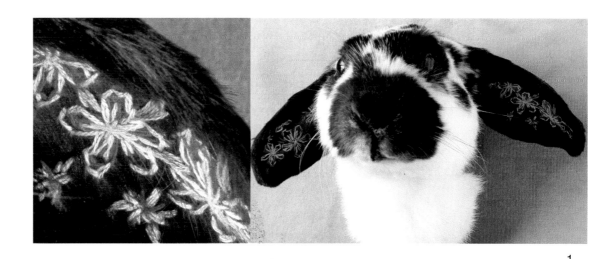

1

2

1. "**Rabbit with Embroi-
dered Ears**"
The ear of rabbit specimen is
embroidered.

2. "**Rabbit with Embroi-
dered Ears** II "
The ear of rabbit specimen is
embedded with beads.

3. "**Sleeping Hare**"
This works is named "Sleeping Hare" and the hare has a
number. The works is inspired
from the fairy tale "The Race
between Turtle and Hare"

3

1

2

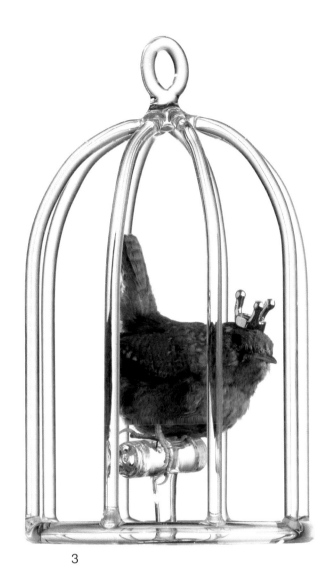

1. "Swan with Human Heart of Glass"
The swan specimen is combined with a human heart of glass.

2. "Protected" mouse in glass hermin on fur Kings-srobe
The cap made of animal furs is decorated with mouse in the glass cover.

3. "WinterKoninkje"
The specimens of bird in the glass cage. Besides the birds with crown, there are ones wearing necklace

4. "Fake"
The specimen of bird on the tree made of glass. The back of the bird is installed with a spring just like the toys with spring.

3

4

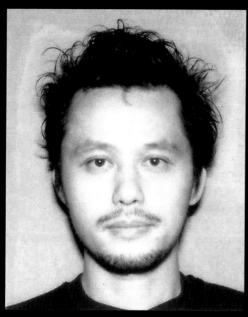

With the help from E&Y, he published the re-cover works with the theme of mediaeval sofa and chair in the Deep Gallery of Tokyo. The same year, taking the opportunity of participation in the LA PLAGED exhibition held by COLETT of Paris, he held the CHRISTOPHE LEMAIRE@WATARU KOMACH Exhibition of Paris and 'le bon marche' department store Exhibition successively and obtain success. Then, he was engaged in the design of Buck T-shirt of Europa tour by which he began the overseas activities formally. Resent years, he held the GOD SAVE THE KATE Exhibition with the title of KATE MOSS in ELECT SHOP THE PINEAL EYE of London in 2005. The same year, he published unique printing works with the ready made style, such as furniture, pottery and ancient costume, which arouse the popularization of collage. He won the BEST TOKYO DESIGN AWARD. In 2006, he held personal exhibition in CIBONE GALLER of Tokyo to appeal the impression of existence.

To express ironic and humorous message through the collage style

Wataru Komachi
Born in Tokyo, Japan

The finished garments gains new life from
the shocking original print

Exhibition at CIBONE GALLERY
The poster of the exhibition held in CIBONE GALLERY of Tokyo in 2006.
His outlook of the world is condensed in the picture which conveys deca–
dence feelings from gray tone.

Pernilla Jansson

From 1998 to 1999, she studied Art in Residental College for Adult Education; from 1999 to 2001, she studied china in Capellagardan of Holland; from 2001 to 2004, she was fully engaged in the study of china and glass in Konstfack University of Art and Craft; in 2005, she studied master's course in the same university. Her talent of art was blooming even though she was still a student. In 2005, her lights that arouse the memory of childhood draw attention widely on the Stockholm Furniture Show.

Her inspiration came from daily life. Her works are not luxurious but tender and full of curiosity to daily life. Her designs direct views to daily life, which is the new subject in the field of Interior Decoration in the 21st century. How will she interpret it? We are full of expectation.

We are looking forward to the flourishing development of the designing style of "directing views to daily life" in the field of Interior Decoration in future.

Pernilla Jansson
Born in Sweden

When the light is enlaced with fringe, monotony changes into elegance.

Top-left: "Fringe on Bulb"
Enlaced with fringe, the soft lighting is full of feminine elegance.

Top-right: "Snap Lamp"
A desk lamp with snap. The fringe can be changed with different atmospheres.

Right: "Suction Cup Lame"
A light with sucking cup can be put at any place you like, such as window and wall.

The "unit of two designers" established their studio in Stockholm, Sweden. They began their designing work in 2001. They focus on the designs of commercial goods-in-promoting. Meanwhile, they also put lots of efforts on the design of merchandise goods and interior decoration.

Both Malin Palm and Aso Ohlsson studied Design in university. After graduation, Malin entered Central Saint Martins College to study Art and Design, and Aso entered Japan Hokkaido Toukai University to study Architecture and Design. The unique natural taste of North Europe, the study of the cities when studying abroad, the craftsmanship derived from nature and the unique synplify of Japan all enrich their works with a unique spice. What make them different from other Swedish designers are the unique charm and feminine decency, delicateness and warmth. Now, their works can be found in Sweden, Finland, Norway, London and Japan.

Their designs are full of decency and warmth.

Design Dessert

Malin Palm: Born 1971 in Kalmar, Sweden /Aso Ohlsson: Born 1967 in Asele, Sweden

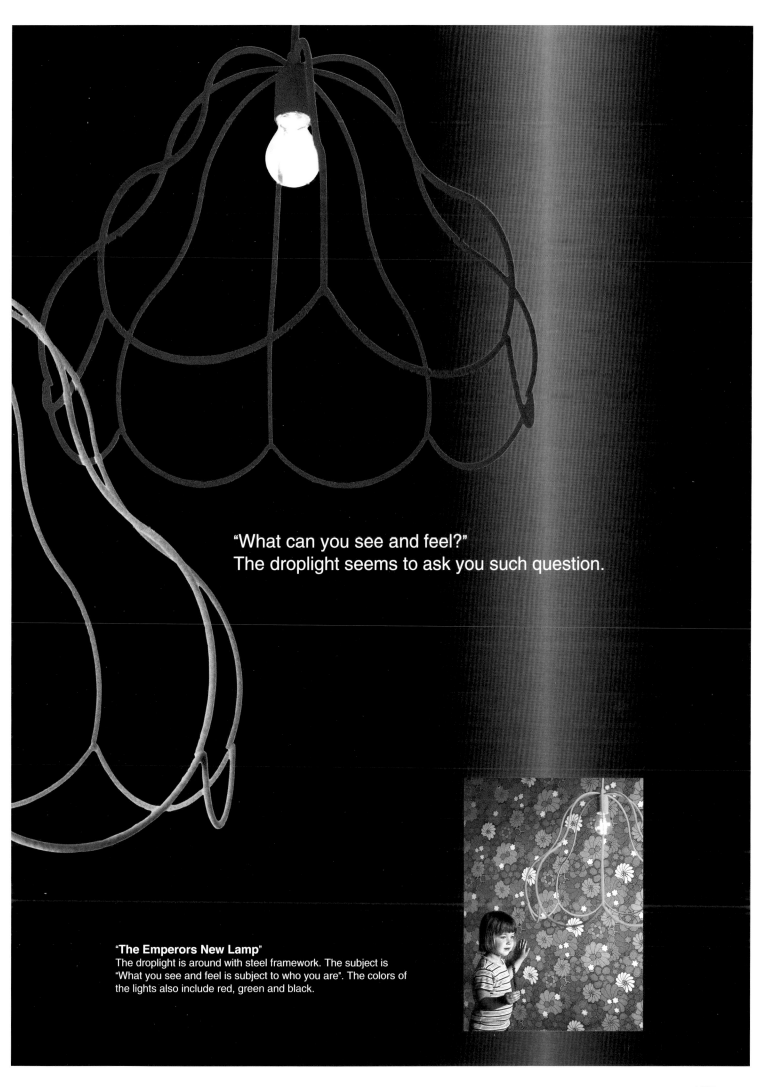

"What can you see and feel?"
The droplight seems to ask you such question.

"The Emperors New Lamp"
The droplight is around with steel framework. The subject is
"What you see and feel is subject to who you are". The colors of
the lights also include red, green and black.

Design Dessert

1

2

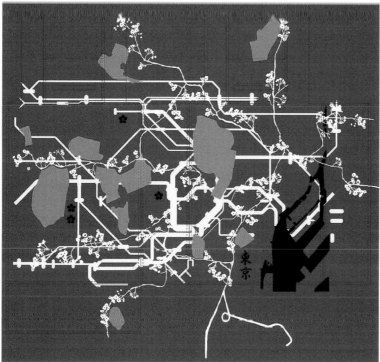

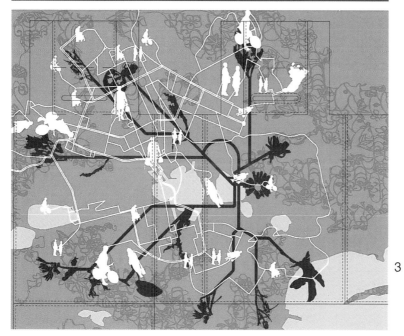

1. "Polo scarf"

It is the combination of tippet and scarf. It is easy to match up with jacket and overcoat. It is a good-idea product in North Europe.

2. "CITY MOSS"

It is also a work that only be imagined by the people living in the cold place.

The queen-sized one allows you to play in it and the small-size one allows you to put your feet in. It has double layers.

3. "REFLEXCITY"

The inspiration for designing the blankets comes from the maps of cities. From top one to last one, they are Moscow, Tokyo and Stockholm.

3

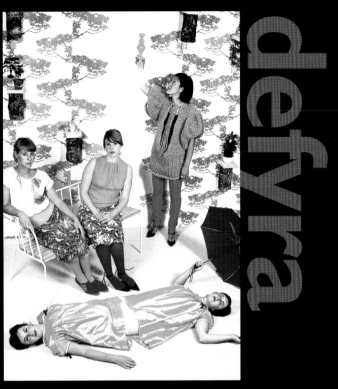

defyra

The "unit of four designers" consists of Anna Hjert, Anna Lang, Sanna Haverinen, and Lena Thak Karlsson. All of them graduate from Beckman's School of Design, one of the most famous schools in Sweden. After graduation in 2001, they held a lot of exhibitions and shows in Sweden, London, Milan, Seoul and Tokyo. As the representatives of young designers from Sweden, they become the focus of attention. In 2003, they became the cractors of art–gallery that holds "Swedish Style".

Most of their works are made of the fragment of furniture and wallpapers. They are full of surre–al humor. They get rid of the Swedish practice of using veneer to show the clean line of works, which conveys a sense of modern design.

However, they said, "though the works are not simple, they are practical, convenient and pleasing".

Their works began with interesting imagina–tion; then they discussed them repeatedly and get rid of the unnecessary parts to make the works more practical. There is no definite di–vision of job between them. The division of job just depends on the characteristics of the works. This working mode produces a lot of colorful works.

A casual smile gives birth to pleasing works.

Defyra
From Sweden

©Helena Blomqvist

Colorful and beautiful works with unique Swedish style.

"Speed Wood stools"
The works was designed jointly by Caroline Heiroth and Stockholm Furniture. It is part of the interior design concept of the hall of Nordic Light Hotel. These are the stools made with the top ends of skis.

Right: "Sushi Zara" for Mono Gallery
These are the series of their porcelain works.

In 1995, she furthered her study in National Konstfack University after graduating from Beckmans–a famous school. Now, she takes Stockholm main working place and also works as the Design Instructor in Sweden, overseas universities and other educational institutes.

She endeavors to unite simplicity with mod–ern technique. Being simple, unadorned and full of joy is right the charm of her works. As the young inheritor of Swedish–style design, besides Sweden, she took part in a lot of ex–hibitions in many countries such as German, Belgium, French and Japan. So far, she has won a lot of awards such as Excellent Swedish Design and Design Plus of German. She has won the big clients like Polrona Frau, E&Y Ja–pan, Offect and David Design. With her future achievements, she will become one of the fa–mous young designers not only in Sweden, but also in the world.

Simplicity × Mordentechnique shows the joy of originality.

Monica Förster
Born 1996 in Stockholm, Sweden

The essence of Swedish Design shown by simplicity and warmth.

"Tray" for Offecct
They are double–deck or three–deck bedstands. The top tray can glide and the lower tray is covered with polyurethane, which has the function of anti–skid.

left: "Sun, Cake, Dot" for Nola
The series of bedstands are made of steel and can be used both inside and outside room. The trays of the bedstands are the same in size and height. The works are trimmed with drawknife. The base of the bedstand can cast a beautiful view.

Monica Förster

Thomas Bernstrand

©Peter Phillips

He studied in Inchbald School of Design in London from 1988 to 1989. Then he went to Denmarks Designskole University, Konstfack University of Arts and Konsthogskolan University of Fine Arts to study Industrial Design, Handicraft and Fine Art.

Initially, Berstrand&Co was a ship factory built by Ernst Bernstrand at the old street in Stocknolm. And then it was moved to Södermalm––an island in the south of Stockholm and became a design company engaged in designing goods, furniture, interior decoration and others. In Södermalm, many young designers live with their brainpower and jointly hold studio. It is an area which is popular with young people. He is 'a designer and inventor' because his works can solve many problems in daily life. The 'globble'—a work showed in the Furniture Exhibition of Stockholm is right an invention for daily life.

As the guidon of Swedish Modern, he has gained many famous Swedish clients such as IKEA, Nola, Swedese, Zero Lighting, etc. Besides, he has Japanese clients—Askul and E&Y as well as Danish client—Muuto, etc. He won the award of 'Designer of Year' of EDIDA/Elle Deco Sweden' and 'Product of year' of Uddabo in Sweden.

An idea man who designs works to eliminate the inconvenience in daily life

Thomas Bernstrand

Born 1965 in Stockholm, Sweden

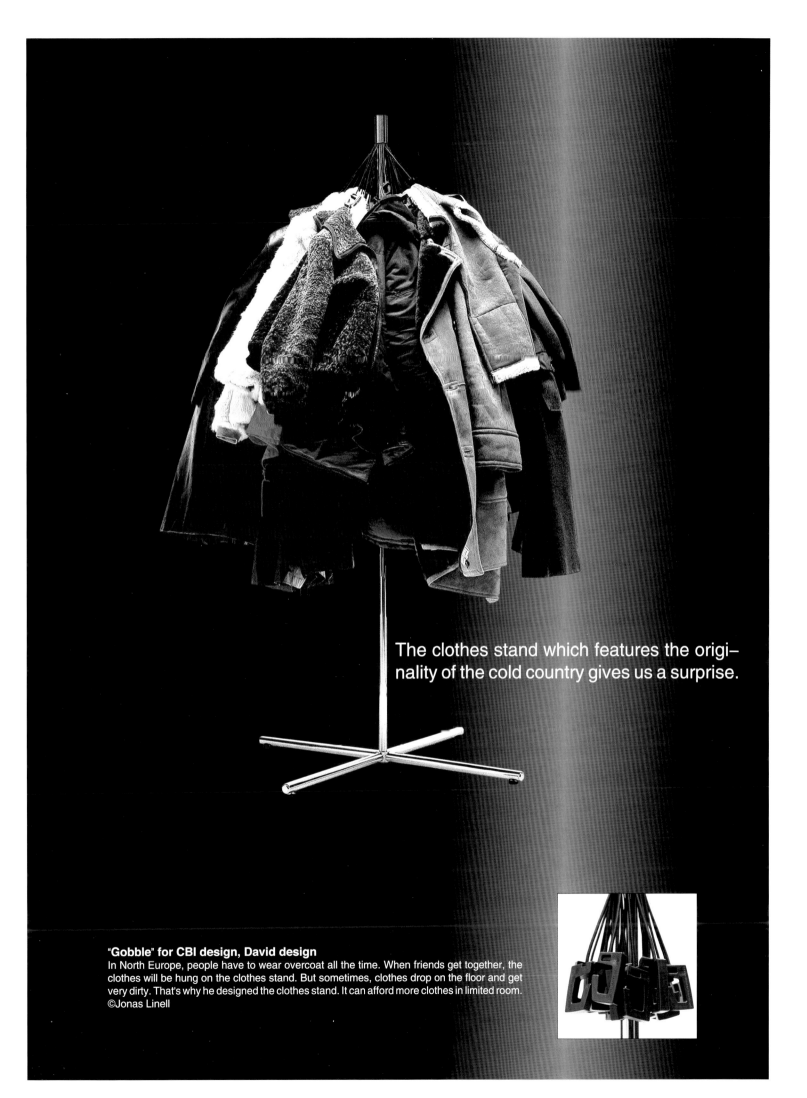

The clothes stand which features the origi–
nality of the cold country gives us a surprise.

"Gobble" for CBI design, David design
In North Europe, people have to wear overcoat all the time. When friends get together, the clothes will be hung on the clothes stand. But sometimes, clothes drop on the floor and get very dirty. That's why he designed the clothes stand. It can afford more clothes in limited room.
©Jonas Linell

Thomas Bernstrand

1

2

3

4

140

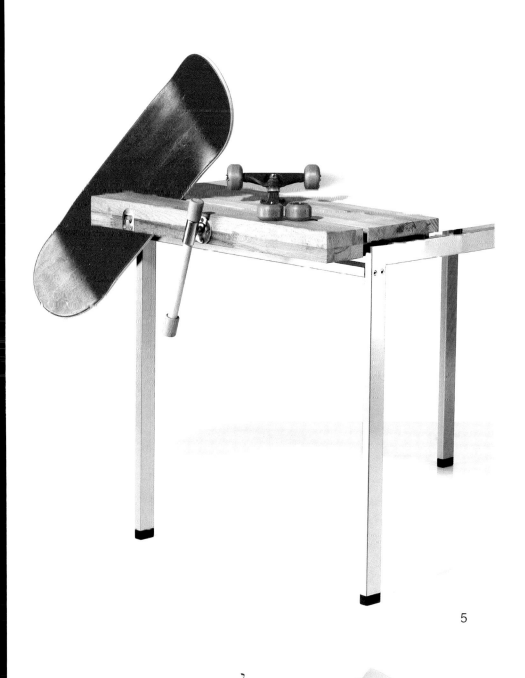

5

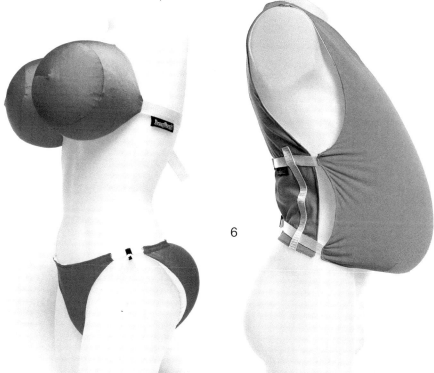

6

1. "Hide" for Zero AB
The floor lamp tries to hide the source of light.
©Zero AB

2. "Even" for Zero AB
The light is slung by wire. Though the wire is not passing through the middle of the light, it still keeps balance. A tricky sense overflows.

3. "Peaple" for Soderbergs Mobler AB, Swedese
Size is not what we pursue. What we want is just a chair which makes us comfortable when we are sitting in it. It meets the client's requirement very well. As the appendage of the chair, the footstool is very flexible and practical.
©Fredrik Sandin Carlson

4. "Time" for Pukeberg
It is a kind of glass made by Hand brown glass bowl--the ancient and traditional technique in Sweden.
©IKEA of Sweden

5. "Uddabo" for Ikea
A dinning table is attached with a planning bench on the one side. It is designed for those people who care much about their dinning tables. The planning bench provides a place for you to cut bread and crab.
©Fredrik Sandin Carlson

6. "Bay watch"/"Sopranos"
A unique and sexy life-jacket.
©Pelle Wahigren

He studied industrial design in Pratt Institute in New York from1992 to1996. Then he went to Denmark National Designing School. In 2001, he set up his own designing studio–– Todd Bracher Studio. He stepped into the field of world interior design with the project "open privacy" in 2001. He made sculpture installation with plywood, carton, and steal tube. More private space can be created with steel tube in public places such as cafes. This analysis method became his unique style later and made his works full of humor. Most of his works are unprecedented. The reason may reside in his experience. He was born in America and lived in Denmark, French and Italy respectively. He is inconsistent with tradition. Now he lives in Italy and takes Italy as beachhead to carry out designing activities.

He designs works for Zanotta, Fritz Hansen, Tronconi, Jaguar and TOM Dixon.

The humor is displayed just by the man who is inconsistent with tradition through the analysis method.

Todd Bracher
Born 1974 in New York, USA

The side tables which are simple but show strong individuality.

"TOD" for Zanotta
The simple side tables with strong individuality are designed with the spatial concept of "beauty mark". The unique feet of the tables are specially designed in consideration that they are often used besides sofa and bed.

Todd Bracher

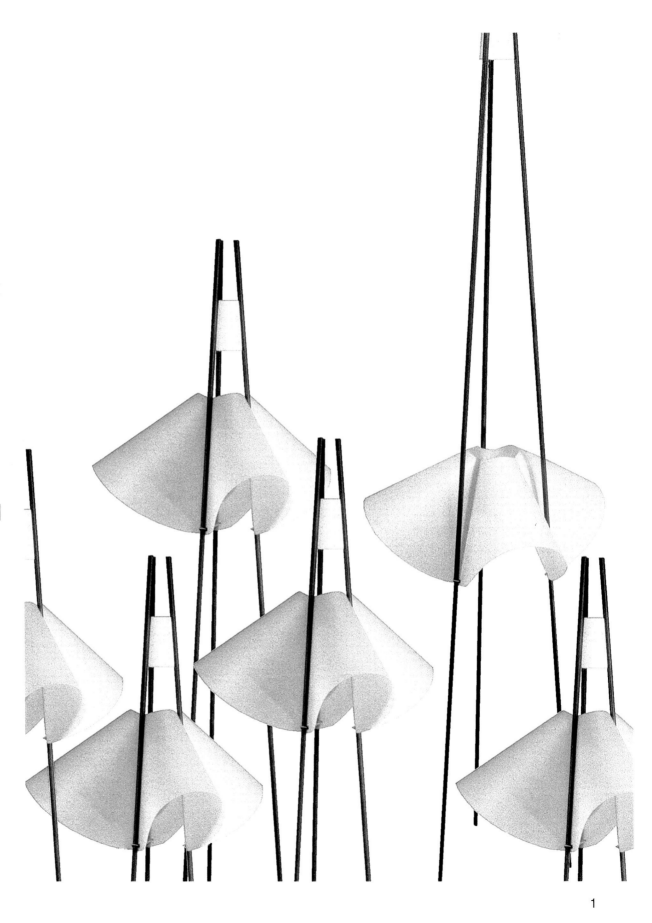

1

2

1. "PENUMBRA"
The shade is made of fiber glass paper. A stand light is made of 3 steel tubes which can be moved up and down.

2. "SOMETHING FROM NOTHING"
The sculpture is made of 1025 hangers. It's one of the works from his free projects, and he could enjoy working on it freely without any plans, trial and error and commercial elements. It was exhibited in Chelsea Hotel in N.Y.

3. "HALO" for Elica
This works is right the elegant combination of industrial application and residential style. The most important feature is simple panel which reflects the luster of the dishes.

3

Todd Bracher

1

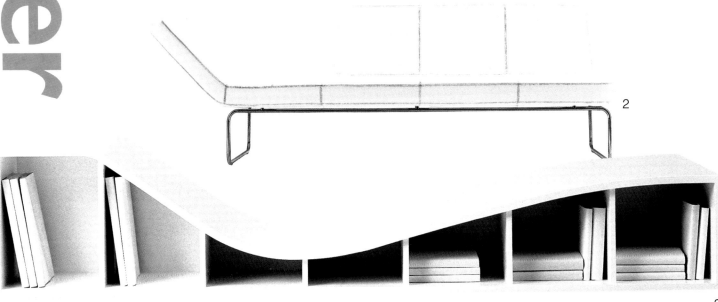

2

3

1. "SLIM" for Zanotta
"Book is not a type of art but an object with aesthetic feeling. The graphic designers work hard to pursue beautiful covers". This works shows homage to the graphic designers. The oblique partition boards help people appreciate the aesthetics of book covers.

2. "Freud" for Zanotta
Sofa, daybed, lounge chair, statuary ....this sofa is flexible to daily life.

3. "Libri Lounge" for Zero First in Tokyo
He said, 'making it a chair that can attract people to read book'. The works was published on Tokyo Designors Block in 2002.

4. "BLOOM"
The works was produced when he lived in Denmark. It was greatly influenced by Denmark. For example, he employed natural ash plywood as material, smooth line and simple form.

4

『 The design in the times without maesrto 』

Kaoro Tashiro

This book shows us part of Italian designs, but it is far from enough. Only few Italian designers are introduced in this book.

As we all know, the competition among the markers of traditional-modeled furniture has been severe all the time in Italy. The international furniture fair and Milano Salon are the world kingdoms of design. During the growth period after the war, the designers with unique designing concept came on scene successively in Italy. Those designers are more distinctive than those in other countries. But few of rising stars came out among their younger generation.

The turning of century is underway. Times have changed a lot, compared with maestro's one. This world is full of materials. Every corner has been designed. Many designers think it unnecessary to design things. But if human beings stopped making objects, the end of the world would come. In dilemma, designers constantly ask themselves how to continue to make objects.

In the Salon of recent years, a lot of makers advocate the individual sense, the division between art and design as well as the saturation of materials. But in fact, they cannot separate design from interior decoration, especially in Italy where numerous outstanding makers gather.

The strategy adopted by the Model Furniture and Product Maker in 1990s is using the overseas star designers. They admit that working with those members will bring an effect of homogenization to designs. What's more, the media give little attention to diligence of the new generation of their domestic designers. It has become a problem. But, this trend comes to a close gradually. This is not the problem which only exists in Italy.

The strong sense of history of Eutopa runs through the designs. It is not throwing away things simply but keeping the memory for things. It's the spiritual base. The designers who breathe different air will have different sense to the time of things. For example, Japan discharges a big amount of waste. But its metabolism is active and productivity is efficient. So the things thrown away are more and more.

Tangible objects will come to an end at last. The designers can prolong the lives of the objects by giving them high quality. The designers should undertake part of the responsibility for building up a healthy market.

As individuals, we expect more and more perfect Italian works which conveys a strong sense of history.

After experiencing the times of maestro and star, we shall pay close attention to the new trend of design.

Profile _____

Kaoro Tashiro
A journalist who focuses on the design, interior decoration and Italian cuisine. Now, he is living in Milano, Italy. He published writing on 『 AXIS 』 first and then worked for 『 Case BRUTUS 』 and 『 Fashionable Communication 』, etc.

Epoch-making stars that continue making legends.

fernando+humberto campana
Tom Dixon
Patricia Urquiola
Marcel Wanders
Claesson Koivisto Rune
Ronan & Erwan Bouroullec
Alfredo Haberli
Hella Jongerious
Carlo Colombo
Tei Shuwa
Björn Dahlström
Jasper Morrison
Philippe Starck
Ron Arad
Antonio Citterio

Based on precise calculation, they add uniqueness and irony to exact design, high craftsmanship and excellent form. They are the top authorities who live in real world but make legendary works in the field of Interior Design. The perfect design of their works shows prominence in the world stage. They will never be limited by works. They will lead the trend of 20th century as well as 21stcentury. They do their best at current works while they continue to challenge for more. Both their designs and living mode will be remembered in the history of Interior Scene.

The design unit is composed of Humberto · Campana who used to be a lawyer and Fernando · Campana who used to be an architect. The unit began their works in San Paulo in 1983. After inspired by the street life of their hometown, they began their activities in the field of furniture and products. Now, they take Estudio campata in San Paulo as beachhead and become active in world interior scene. Their works, which are made of materials of daily life and industrial discards, have drawn the attention widely. Artistic furniture became well-known as their names were well-known to the world. Several of their works have been published by Edra in Italy such as the fasteners used for bell bed and "favela" –a chair made of numerous wood chips. At present, their main clients are Edra, Cappellini etc. Their design of furniture overthrows the old designing concept and brings great impact to interior world. They save no effort to bring their creativity into full play and equip furniture with practicability. The works, which are produced in the interstice between design and art haunted by messages, bring people a strong sense of impact and remain unforgettable. As guidons of Brasilia design, the two brothers took part in various international exhibitions such as "idea house" on Koln International Furniture Exhibition in 2005 and another exhibition held by Brazil Embassy in Japan in 2005. The brothers activities which contain endless possibilities arouse the attention worldwide.

fernando+humberto campana

A "brothers unit" which gets inspiration from Brazil—their motherland and creates unique design.

Fernando+humberto campana

Fernando : Born 1961 humberto: Born in 1953 in Sãn Paulo, Brazil

A mirror table made of the fragments of mirrors arouses
the imagination for the Sao Paulo Street.

"Brasilia" table for Edra
A table assembled with the fragments of mirror at random was published by Edra on Milano Salon in 2006.
© Edra

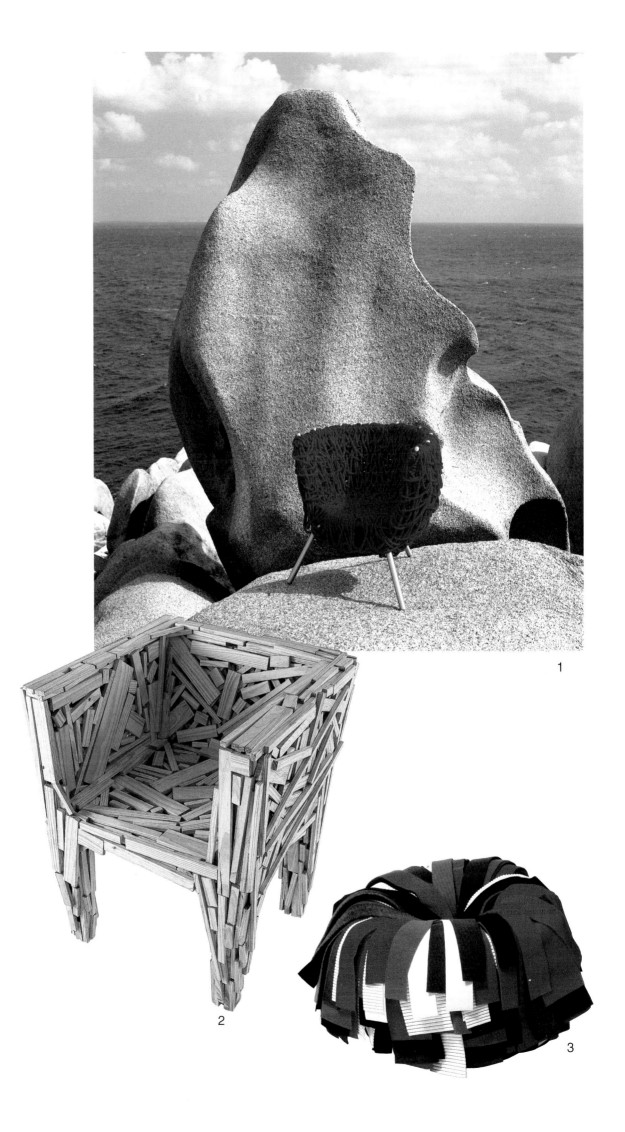

fernando+humberto campana

1

2

3

1. "Vermelha" armchair for Edra
The armchair is made of a stainless steel framework and enlaced with robe. The inspiration of the works came from the robe sold on the street market in Sao Paulo. This piece was mentionable after he stepped into the field of interior design and challenged international design scene later.

2. "Favela" armchair for Edra
The armchair is assembled with a lot of fragments of nature trees. This way of making is close to the way of making little house with animal glue by people in the Slum Street in Brazil. No two works are identical because they are handicrafts. This limitation in number is the special feature of his works.

3. "Sushi" for Edra
The chair is made by intertwining different kinds of fabric and other materials together, and then adding flexible polyurethane materials and fabric tube. The outside part looks as if it is made of colorful sheets. It shows the shape of natural corolla after being displayed.

4. "Kaiman Jacare" for Edra "Aster Papposus" for Edra
The cushion sofa was published in Edra showroom of MILANO SALONE in 2006. It looks like a horrific creature which is floating in the deep sea and give people a strong impact.
© Edra

5. "Jenette" chair for Edra
It is made of polyurethane material with firm metal core. The back of the chair costs 900 flexible stalks which are made of PVC. Reclining on the back will be comfortable.
© Edra

6. "Carallo" chair for Edra
It is a hand-knitted irregular steel wire chair. It is a delicate decoration that can be used both in and out of door.
© Edra

Tom Dixon was born in Tunisia. His father is English and his mother is the hybrid from French and Latvian. When he was 4–year–old, he moved to England and studied in London. He once went to study in Chelsea Art School; however, he left the school after 6 months due to bike accident. Later, as a base player, he began his music activities, but he quit due to bike accident again. Then he studied the technique Practicing Bumper himself. This greatly influenced his later designs.

Most of his early works in workshop are the converted products of recycled metal and discards. Breaking, adjusting and remaking the scrap metal are just meeting his brash character. This experience made him turn to industry. He held various exhibitions in those years. In 1980s, he was found by Cappellini. He became known to the world after his "S chair" was published by Cappellini. Now, the chair has become the permanent collection of MOMA. He set up Euro Lounge in 1994 and made a lot of plastic products. He won the Millennium Mark Award with "the jack light" in 1997. He was appointed as design head of Habitat in England. As creative director, he made great achievements for the reformation of finance. His design and reformation achievements were acknowledged by the people around the world. In 2000, he won OBE. He founded his own design company in 2001 and began to publish his works in the exhibitions held on Milano Salone and London Design Museum, etc. All of his new works became new topics in the field of international design.

With rare talent that challenged the tradition, the English genius surprised the world constantly.

Tom Dixon
Born 1959 in Sfax, Tunisia

Icon works of Tom Dixon, mirror ball lamp
which is often used all over the world.

"Mirror Ball"
It is a mirror lamp with the unique form of chapped bubble gum. The material is plastics which are
processed with metallic processing technique. Adding mirror and shade makes it more beautiful. It
is often used in shops and restaurants. There are also mini types of table lamps.

Tom Dixon

1

2

1. "Cone light"
The lamp has pendant, floor and stand as well as multi-functions. The reflected cone-shaped rays look like the sun-ray and radiate evenly. The front part of the surface is composed of acry diffuser plate.

2. "Tower"
Golden dynamic object.

3. "Fat spot"
The floor light is made of poly-carbonate materials and radiates the rays in the form of beam. Its prism-shaped shade is its special feature.

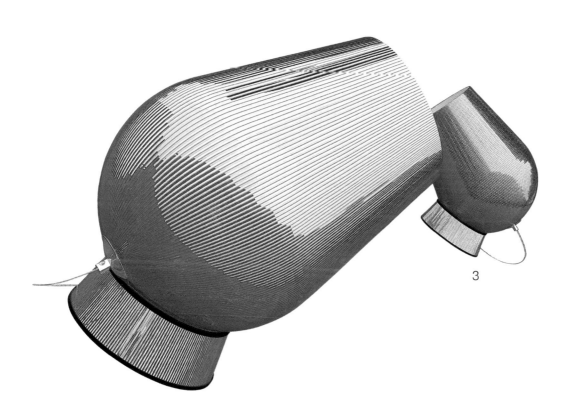

3

1

2

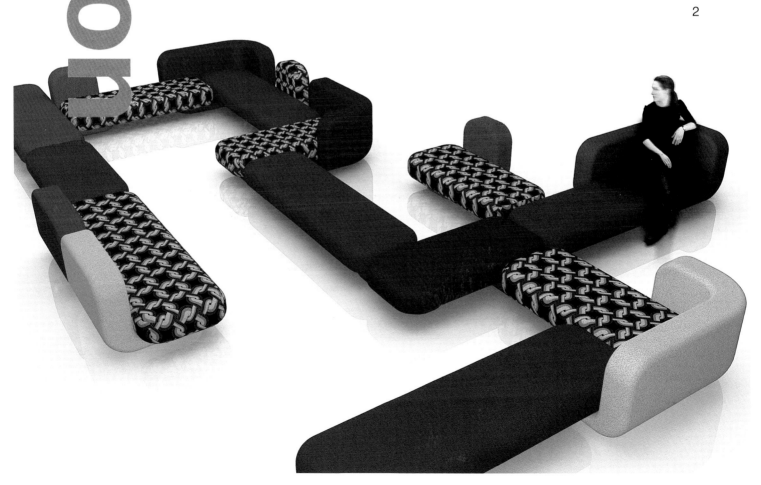

Tom Dixon

3

1. "Tall chair"
It is a chair with high back and unique expression. It was published on Milano Salone in 2005.

2. "Soft System"
The Sofa System is made of wood in the form of multi density. It can be used either at home or public space because its size is flexible.

3. "Link easy chair"
It is a link easy chair decorated by white power coat. The cushion can be fit according to your need. The thin steel wires bring joy to people (with little impact).

4. "Wire series"
It is a popular wire series of dining chairs which are suitable for outdoor use. In addition, another version is made by power coating including two series i.e. coat hook and coat rack.

4

161

Patricia Urquiola

She studied in Architecture Department in Madrid Polytechnic and Milan Polytechnic University and graduated in 1989. Under the instruction of Achille Castiglioni and Eugenio Bettinellihis—her tutors, she worked as an assistant in Milano Industrial University from 1990 to 1992. From 1990 to 1996, she worked with Vico Magistretti in product development department of De Padova. In 1993, she founded a studio with M de Renzio and E. Ramerino to deal with some interior projects concerning construction, restaurant and showroom. From 1996 to 2000, being registered in studio lissioni and associates, the studio could took part in such projects as Alessi, Antares-flos, Artelano, Boffi, Cappellini, Cassina and Kartell. Meanwhile, she herself collaborated with other companies such as B&B, Karell, Molteni&Cc, Moroso, Da Driade, etc. In 2001, she founded her own studio. It mainly dealt with product development, exhibition-design, art direction and construction. On Milano Salone held in 2004, her works were published by ten companies and attracted great attention. Now, she takes Milano as beachhead to begin her activities. Her design works which show her personality arouse the attention from the world and won the offers from lots of main makers. She is now one of the most famous designers.

She has been appraised as wonder woman by the makers.

Patricia Urquiola
Born 1961 in Oviedo, Spain

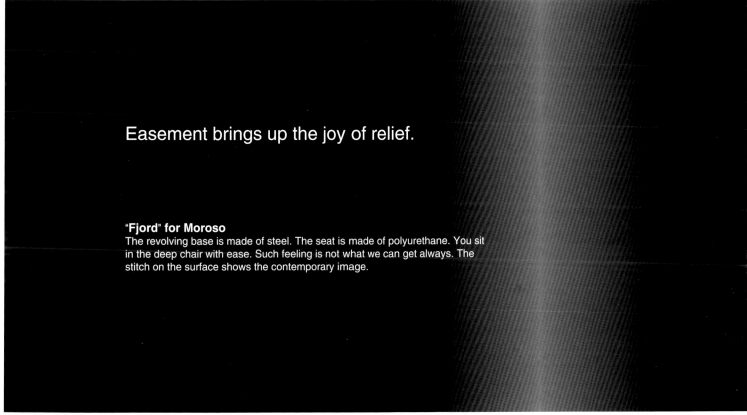

Easement brings up the joy of relief.

"Fjord" for Moroso
The revolving base is made of steel. The seat is made of polyurethane. You sit in the deep chair with ease. Such feeling is not what we can get always. The stitch on the surface shows the contemporary image.

1

2

1. "Digitable" for B&B Italia

The holes on the side table are made with water jet. The 'U'-shaped curve is its special feature.

2. "Lazy" for B&B Italia

The B&B collection has four types of chairs such as arm chair, bench and high back rest. There are also outdoor patterns of designs.

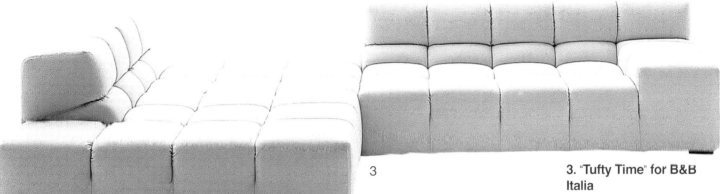

3

3. "Tufty Time" for B&B Italia

The name of sofa system of "Tufty" has the meaning of 'a lot of houses'. The sofa system is a module type that is made of a lot of ottomans. They can form a comfortable space for users.

4. "smock" for Moroso

The sofa with the style of hammock. It was published in Idea House of Koln International Furniture Exhibition. The ring-shaped armrest and wave-shaped side convey elegance. The frame is made of stainless chromium and painted with lacquer (the name of a kind of paint). The cushion is made of goose feather.

4

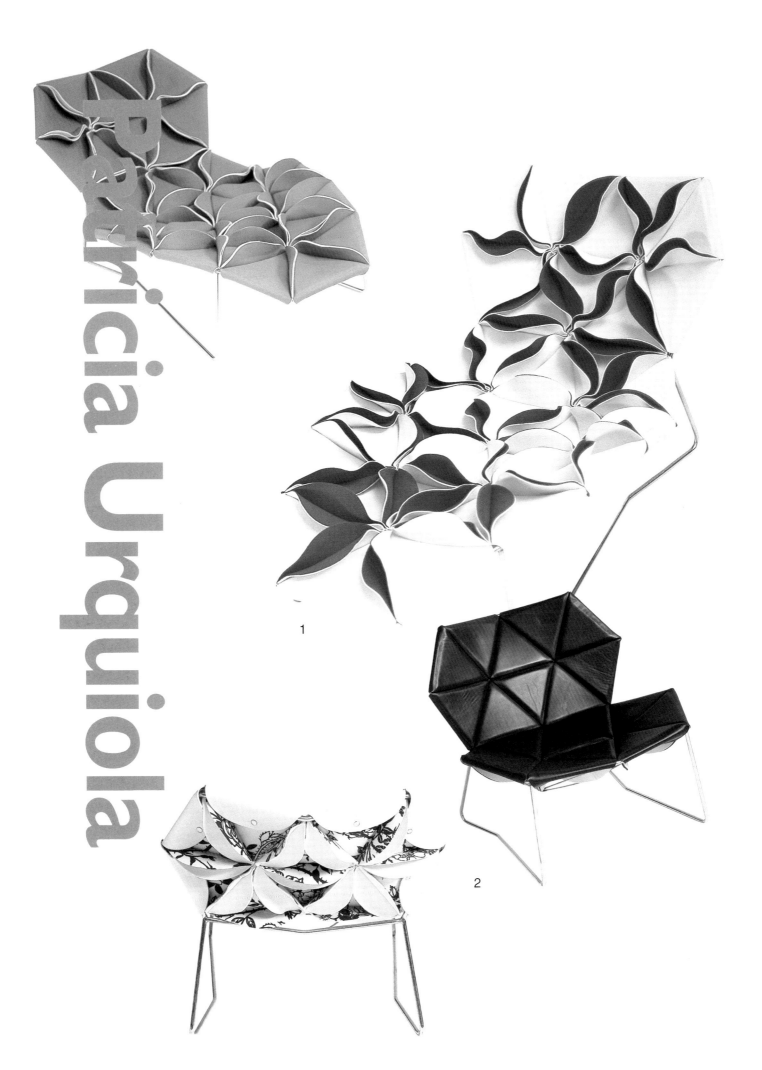

Patricia Urquiola

1

2

1,2. "antibodi" for Moroso

There are two types--davenport and lounge chair. They are made of the fabric of wool felt and leather. The wool felt is soft, so the flower is showed clearly. The uneven surface seems to place people in the garden with enchanting and romantic atmosphere. She is good at feminine design. These are the works which show her true value.

3. "By side" for Bisazza

It is mosaic tile screen with the size of 240×206. It is composed of frames with different sizes. Each frame is moveable. As her main works, it was published in the showroom of Bisazza on Milano Salone in 2006.

4. "T-table" for Kartell

The side table is made by the perfect combination of her creativity and the outstanding technique of plastic furniture maker and kartell. Though it is easy to be mistaken for technique research, result of experiment and glass-carving in vision and touch, it is a decorative elegant table top.

5. "Caboche" for Foscarini

She designed the suspension lamp in cooperation with Eliana Gerotto. The transparent balls are made of acryl materials with the decoration of white mark. The light from the ball can achieve the effect of expanding the space. Besides, it looks as if a big bubble contains a lot of small bubbles. It is so beautiful.

3

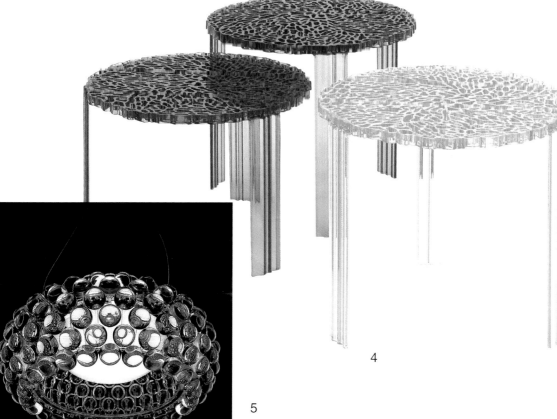

4

5

He majored in 3D in Arnhem Art School and graduated from the school in 1988. He took Amsterdam as beachhead to begin his activities. In 1992, he founded design studio with others and began publishing works. KLM Royal Dutch Airlines and Apple were his clients. Meanwhile, he was one of the members at the early stage of Droog Design. In 1995, he founded his own studio--Wanders Wonders, and began to collaborate with first-class companies such as Cappllini and British Airway. In 1996, his work 'Kontted Chair' which was published by Cappellini was selected as permanent collection. Then he was known to the world because of his appeal of Dutch design. He aroused the attention of the world because he turned the materials in daily life into the works full of unique charm. Besides above-mentioned clients, he also collaborates well with Bisazza, Moroso, Polidorm, Flos, Mandarina Duck, b&b Ltakia, Cassina and Boffi. Now he has become one of the most popular designers.

In 2001, he became the Creative Director of Moooi—a famous maker which gathered famous designers from all over the world. He is dedicated to displaying the charm of Dutch design to the world together with other young rising designers such as Maaten Baas.

He is the man who makes the power of Dutch design known to the world and carries on with the charisma of Dutch design.

Marcel Wanders
Born 1963 in Boxtel, Netherlands

Audio system with visual enjoyment.

"pandora" / "mathilda" / "domino" for HE
The AV system was published on IFA 2005 Exhibition of Household Appliances and Electronics in Berlin.
"Pandora" is a wireless speaker which combines the table of woofer and 2.1 stereo sound. "Mathilda" is
antenna which is used to delete the sound of Notebook PC and Mp3. It can be used with Pandora and Do-
min at the same time. Domino is an ultra-thin speaker system. It receives audio signal and displays sound.
©Maarten van Houten

change

1

2

3

Marcel Wanders

4

5

1. "Bottoni and Bottoni wang" for moooi

The simple sofa has slim steel feet. The originality resides in the tracery fabric on the back. It can be detached with the button and be changed in patterns such as Gobelins, flower motif, metallic geometric and in the material of fur according to the season or the interior change.

2, 3. "New Antiques" for Cappellini

The classic furniture is made of wood and painted with various colors. The Form, carving and pattern of the designed 'antique' reanimate the modernism. The white type is newly published in 2006.

4. "set up shades limited edition" for moooi

It is a limited edition for '5'. It is a type that is made of pattern fabric.
©Maarten van Houten

5. "set up shades" for moooi

The overlapping makes the lamp shade unique. The works is composed of 5-7 shades. The technique of Pvc/cotton laminating makes the work radiate soft light.
©Maarten van Houten

Marcel Wanders

1

2

174

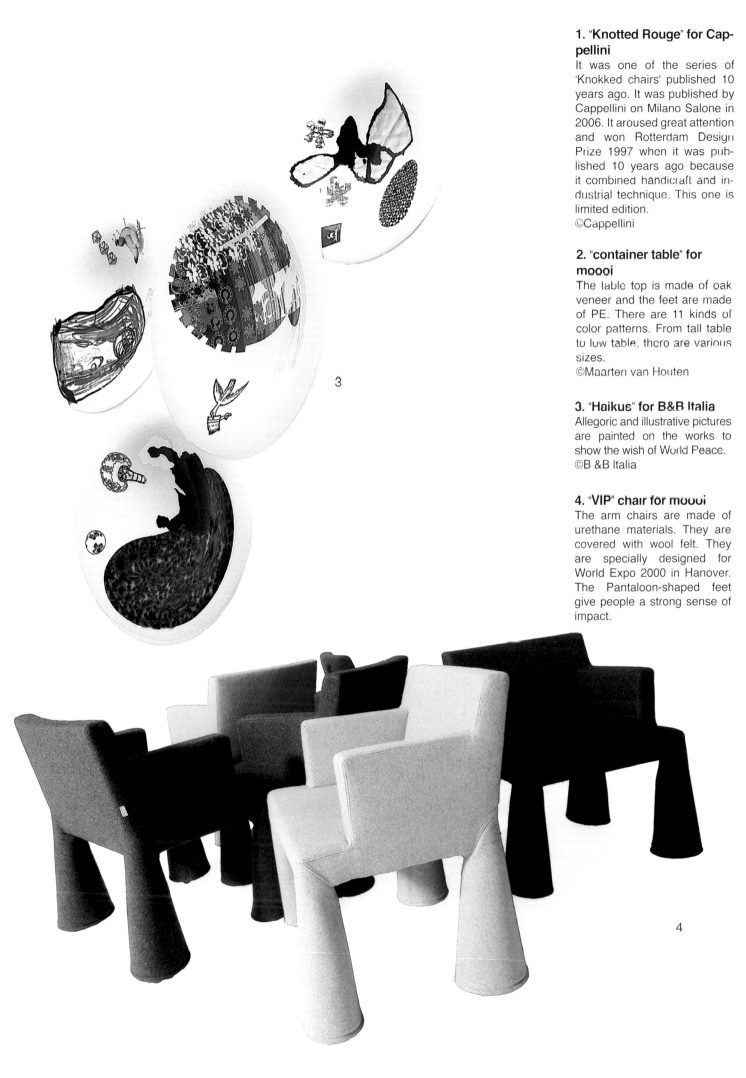

1. "Knotted Rouge" for Cappellini

It was one of the series of 'Knokked chairs' published 10 years ago. It was published by Cappellini on Milano Salone in 2006. It aroused great attention and won Rotterdam Design Prize 1997 when it was published 10 years ago because it combined handicraft and industrial technique. This one is limited edition.
©Cappellini

2. "container table" for moooi

The table top is made of oak veneer and the feet are made of PE. There are 11 kinds of color patterns. From tall table to low table, there are various sizes.
©Maarten van Houten

3. "Haikus" for B&B Italia

Allegoric and illustrative pictures are painted on the works to show the wish of World Peace.
©B &B Italia

4. "VIP" chair for moooi

The arm chairs are made of urethane materials. They are covered with wool felt. They are specially designed for World Expo 2000 in Hanover. The Pantaloon-shaped feet give people a strong sense of impact.

3

4

The designing unit consists of Marten Claesson (the left one), Eero Koivisto (the middle one) and Ola Rune (the right one) . In 1995, they founded a designing studio–Claesson Koivisto Rune in Sweden to deal with construction design, industrial design and designs in other fields. Claesson studied in Konstfack University College of Arts in Stockholm and then he studied engineering, construction and product–design in many universities. Now, he works as a freelancer–writer and instructor of construction &design. Besides, he deals with the publication of newspapers and magazines. Koivisto studied in Konstfack University College of Arts too. Besides, he studied in the University of Arts & Design in Helsinki and construction and furniture design in other universities. Now, he takes Stockholm as beachhead to begin his lecture in Canada, America and Mexico. Rune studied in Konstfack University College of Arts in Stockholm, Southwark College of Arts & Design in London, the Royal Academy of Arts in Gopenhagen and Stockholm School of Arts. Now, he is a lecturer of Beckman's Design—one of the most famous school in Stockholm.

As for furniture, the unit has a lot of clients such as Asplund, Boffi, Cappellini, David Design, E&Y, Thonet, Franc franc and Offecct. As for architecture field, they work for Swedish Embassy in Berlin, Sony Music in Stockholm, Gucci, Louis Vuitton, Air Euro Shop in Scandinavia and Asplund shop. They become the representatives of the design of North Europe and arouse great attention.

Claesson Koivisto Rune

Swedish architect unit with the creativity of $1+1+1=\infty$.

Claesson Koivisto Rune
From Sweden

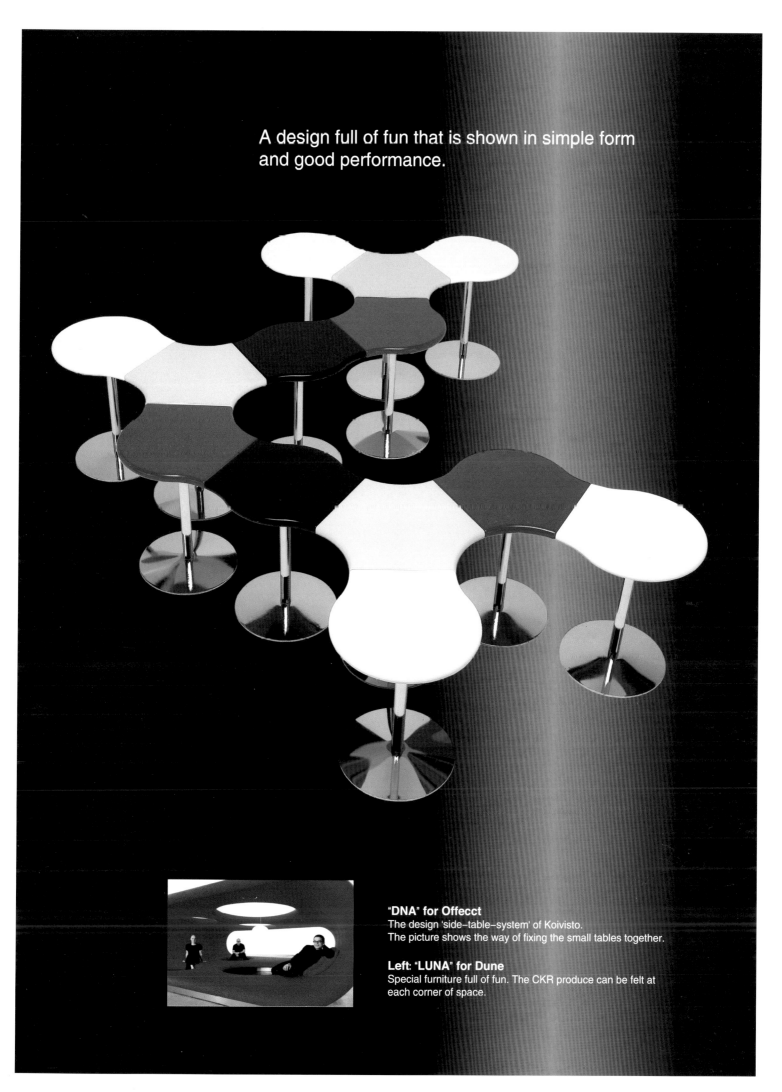

A design full of fun that is shown in simple form
and good performance.

"DNA" for Offecct
The design 'side–table–system' of Koivisto.
The picture shows the way of fixing the small tables together.

Left: "LUNA" for Dune
Special furniture full of fun. The CKR produce can be felt at
each corner of space.

1

2

182

1. "Float" for Offecct
The arm-chair & sofa-system designed by Koivisto.

2. "WINDOW" for Offecct
A coffee-table designed by Koivisto. A table top with window is unique.

3

3. "SFERA Chair" for SFERA FURNITURE
A special cutting sofa made of sheet. The delicate pattern makes beautiful shadow.

4. "RODRIGO" for Swedese
A chair designed by Claesson. The simple and lovely silhouette makes unique expression.

4

Claesson Koivisto Rune

1

2

3

184

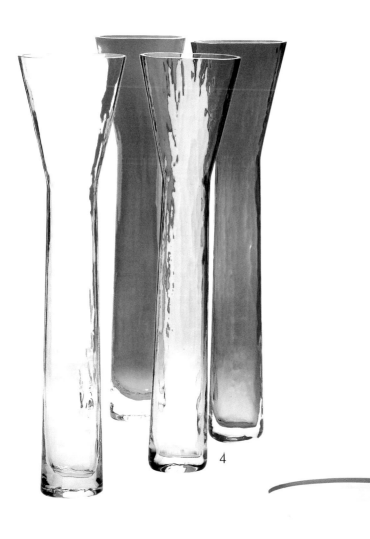

4

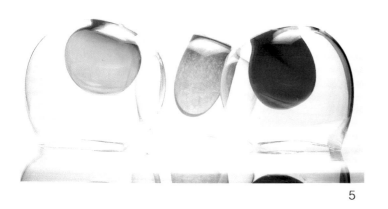

5

1. "BEND" for Swedese
Chair, bench, stool & table designed by Claesson. The tender line of the wood material is right the design of Swedish style.

2. "OMNI" for Swedese
Arm-chair & foot-stool designed by Claesson and Koivisto. The specially-designed seat and the angle of head-rest make you feel comfortable when sitting. It is one of representative works for Swedese

3. "Gahan" for David Design
A dining–table designed by Koivisto.

4. "Liljia" for SKRUF
Flower-base designed by Claesson.

5. "Mum" for SKRUF
Flower-base designed by Koivisto. It has a striking contrast with Lijia designed by Claesson.

6. "SEESAW" for De Vecchi
Solt & Pepper-shaker. When putting them on table, their wiggly movement is so lovely.

7. "Spool" for Lucente
Besides this floor-lamp, there are also pendant-light and table-lamp.

6

7

©Morgane Le Gall

Ronan (older brother) began his designing career after graduation from Ecole Nationale Des Arts Decoratif. Erwan (the younger brother) assisted him when Erwan was still a student of Ecole Des Beaux-arts. From 1999, they began to work together.

In 1997, the Disintegrated Kitchen published on Salon du Meuble de Paris took Giulio Cappellini's fancy, and then they collaborated with Cappellini in many ways. In 2000, they set about shop-design for the new collaboration with Issey Miyake. In the same year, they met the chairman of Vitra. In 2002, they published the office furniture system known as "Joyn". They enjoyed good collaboration with makers. The feature of their works is that they challenge the current concept and suggest a new relationship between the works and the users. Now, they have a lot of clients such as Vitra, Cappellini, Issey Miyake, Magis, Ligne Roset and Habitat. They won a lot of prizes such as "Creator of the Year" on Salon du Meuble de Paris in 2002; "New Designer Award" on International Furniture Exhibition in New York in 1999 and "designer of the year" in ELLE DECO in Japan. Many of their works are the permanent collections in MOMA, Centre Pompidou of Paris and London Design Museum.

Ronan & Erwan Bouroullec

The Relationship Between The Works And User Life-style's creator

Ronan & Erwan Bouroullec

Ronan: Born 1971 Erwan : Born 1976 in Quimper, France

"Joyn" with new concept brings renovation to Office-system.

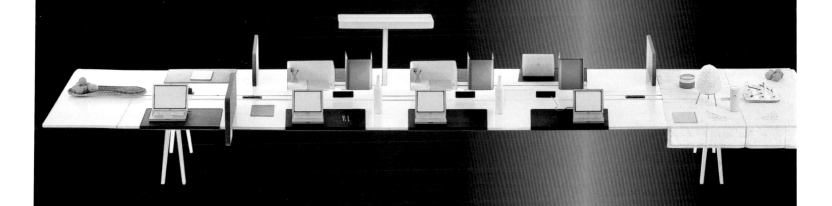

"Joyn Office-system" for Vitra
The universal working system is made by the brothers with Vitra Company—which has a history of 40 years in making office-system. Because it is simple, it can be used in many ways. Partition is appendix. If you remove the partition, it becomes a meeting-table. The renovated office-system with new functions has been highly appraised.
© Vitra

He was born in Buenos Aires, Argentina in 1964 and moved to Switzerland in 1977. He studied industrial-design in Hochschule für Bildende Künste Braunschweig and graduated in 1991. From 1988, he began to hold a lot of exhibitions for Museum fur Gestaltung which belonged to Schule fur. In 1993, he founded Schule fur Studio and then worked for reading-design companies such as Alias, Authentics, Edra, Driade, Luceplan, Thonet, Zanotta etc. As an international industrial designer, he is one of the most popular persons. He teaches in Schule fur design and Domus Academy in Milan, etc now.

What he stresses is not formal or fashionable appearance but viewing things with new concept in daily life. As a result, a lot of new and definite ideas come out. The feature of his works is cheerfulness, humanity, glaringness, beautifulness and the penetration into the concept of the things. This is why he often says 'observing things is the best way for thinking'.

Now, he designs for Bd Ediciones de Diseno, Cappellini, Classicon, Littala, Joop, Leitner, Moroso, Offecct and Volvo. He held a lot of exhibitions around the whole Europe and won a lot of prizes. He is a leader of the young designers.

Alfredo Haberli

The design standard for 21st century under expectation. The top leader of the Industrial-Design field.

Alfredo Haberli

Born 1964 in Buenos Aires, Argentina

Keen observation leads to the masterpiece of wire–chair
with high performance and designing breakthrough.

"Nais" wire chair for CLASSICON
It is made of titanium wire. Generally, the seat of a chair does not rock. Nais reduces the
amount of wires to make the chair rock up and down and make people feel comfortable.

©Louise Dillgert

She studied Industrial Design in Eindhoven and graduated in 1993. She designed porcelain stool for Rosenthal and Droog Design. He made porcelain pot, jar, stool and chair for New York Dana Karan and Cappellini and aroused the attention from markers. In 2000, she founded her own company—Jongerius Lab.

The main feature of her works is the integration of polyurethane, latex, steel, felt, porcelain, glass, cloth, plastics, bronze and gold. As for the architecture, the combination of raw materials and technique reformation is the main feature of her works. In these works, she tries hard to keep the balance between the mass–produced industrial products without added value and the unique value of the handicraft showing identity. This shows her concept that "the cost and expenses on the works do not mean the value of the works".

Some of her works are limited editions. She has a lot of clients such as Maharam, Swarovski, Royal Tichelaar, Hermes, Ikea and Vitra. Besides, her works become parts of the collection in many national/international art galleries.

Now, she designs home collection for Vitra, the interior decoration for Maharam and curtain & beddings for Spaarne hospital in Amsterdam.

She seeks for the meaning and value of design through handmade porcelain works.

Hella Jongerius
Born 1963 in De Meern, Netherlands

Keen observation leads to the masterpiece of wire–chair
with high performance and designing breakthrough.

"Nais" wire chair for CLASSICON
It is made of titanium wire. Generally, the seat of a chair does not rock. Nais reduces the
amount of wires to make the chair rock up and down and make people feel comfortable.

1

2

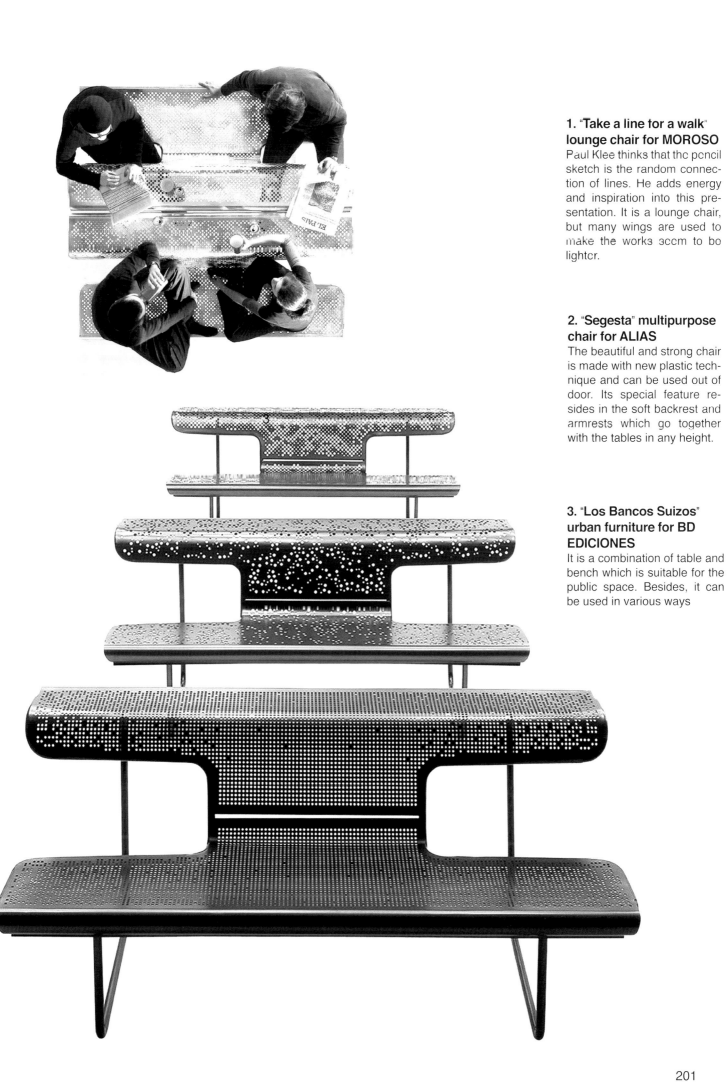

1. "Take a line for a walk" lounge chair for MOROSO

Paul Klee thinks that the pencil sketch is the random connection of lines. He adds energy and inspiration into this presentation. It is a lounge chair, but many wings are used to make the works seem to be lighter.

2. "Segesta" multipurpose chair for ALIAS

The beautiful and strong chair is made with new plastic technique and can be used out of door. Its special feature resides in the soft backrest and armrests which go together with the tables in any height.

3. "Los Bancos Suizos" urban furniture for BD EDICIONES

It is a combination of table and bench which is suitable for the public space. Besides, it can be used in various ways

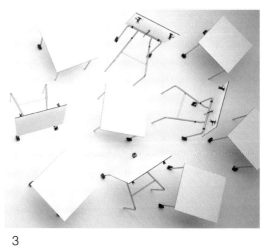

Alfredo Haberli

1

2 3

202

4

5

6

1. "Gordon" low chair for TRUNZ
The light and comfortable arm-chair which can be used out of the door. This works is easy to be produced because it is bent with laser/razor and fixed with rivet.

2. "Ginger Stool" barstool with shelf for BD EDIICIO-NES
The name of the works 'Ginger' came from the name of a Jap-anese restaurant. This stool is more convenient and comfort-able than barstool used in the public space because there is a shelf under the seat.

3. "Move It" multipurpose table for THONET
The works consists of a table-top and four legs which look like wheels. It is supported by gas spring. Several tables can be piled up like the trolley used in airport. In this way, more spaces can be saved.

4. "Pick Up" chair, walking aid and storage in one for OFFECCT
A chair with multi-functions. Child can sit on it, push it, or play with toys on it. Once, he saw his son grasp the stool when he is about to fall down at his first walking. The inspira-tion of this work came from that scene.

5. "Solitaire" low chair with table for OFFECCT
A chair made of single kind of material. One type is attached with a small table. The other type is a deep one which can be used as a shelf.

6. "Sofa TT" upholstered sofa for ALIAS
The sofa is made of polyure-thane materials and steel, so it is very soft. The legs are made of aluminum. It is simple but convenient and comfortable.

Alfredo Haberli

1

2

204

1. "Tris" candlelight for IITTALA

Candle holder in the shape of triangle. The depth is different. The soft light radiates from the charming shape.

2. "Essence" range of glasses for IITTALA

It is one of his works for II-TALA-the most important client. His family dealt in restaurant and hotel. So, the works is useful for his family. For him, it is works that activates his personal knowledge. The width of the wineglass demonstrates the balance between tradition and modern. It can be used on the formal occasion or in daily life. A glass without stem is shot glass, but it can be used as table wine. The pink color on the wineglass in the picture is the color of the wine which is reflected on the glass.

3. "Kids'Stuff" tableware, glasses and cutlery for IITTALA

Kids' tableware and cutlery. He drew on the memory of his childhood and found that, compared with adult, the kid is cleverer; besides, kids' fantasy is not universal. The care can be found in a little blunt knife and the plate without edge. He hopes that the kid who had used this set of tableware will say that 'your Kids' Stuff' is my best memory of my childhood' after he grows up.

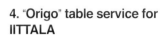

4. "Origo" table service for IITTALA

The concept of 'Origo' can make the production of the daily-used tableware easier according to different needs. The stacking on the bottom is used to fix the cup and bowl. The decorative factors are just appendants.

©Louise Billgert

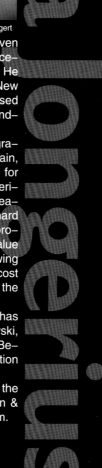

She studied Industrial Design in Eindhoven and graduated in 1993. She designed porcelain stool for Rosenthal and Droog Design. He made porcelain pot, jar, stool and chair for New York Dana Karan and Cappellini and aroused the attention from markers. In 2000, she founded her own company—Jongerius Lab.

The main feature of her works is the integration of polyurethane, latex, steel, felt, porcelain, glass, cloth, plastics, bronze and gold. As for the architecture, the combination of raw materials and technique reformation is the main feature of her works. In these works, she tries hard to keep the balance between the mass-produced industrial products without added value and the unique value of the handicraft showing identity. This shows her concept that "the cost and expenses on the works do not mean the value of the works".

Some of her works are limited editions. She has a lot of clients such as Maharam, Swarovski, Royal Tichelaar, Hermes, Ikea and Vitra. Besides, her works become parts of the collection in many national/international art galleries.

Now, she designs home collection for Vitra, the interior decoration for Maharam and curtain & beddings for Spaarne hospital in Amsterdam.

She seeks for the meaning and value of design through handmade porcelain works.

Hella Jongerius

Born 1963 in De Meern, Netherlands

Warmth and beauty of the handicraft
that are confided by animals.

"Nympenburg Sketches" for Nympenburg Porzelann
The works with the hope to show the refinement of handicraft. The one with porcelain
animal is very artful. In order to show that one is different from the other, the works are
carved with serial number.

Hella Jongerius

1

2

3

4

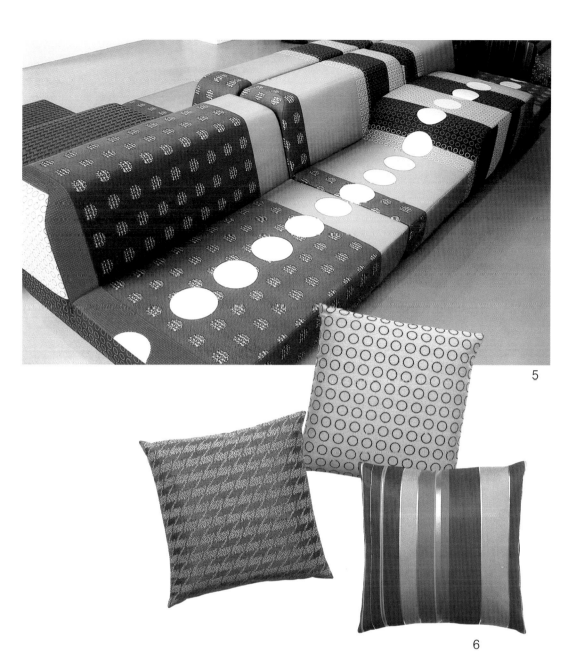

1. "Delfts blue jug" for Koninklijke Tichelaar Makkum

A jug with simple color of 'B-set' is added with a copper handle. The handle is fixed with plastic fasteners.

2,4. "B-set dinner service" for Royal Tichelaar Makkum

In order to endue the plate and cup with identity, irregular variation is added to daily-used tableware. This works became the collection of Drooq Design.

3. "Delfts blue bowl" for Koninklijke Tichelaar Makkum

It is one of Delft in Detail shown on Curat Exhibition in 2001 Compared with 'B-set', the series focus more on decorative theme. In the inner side, it is a hand-painted ancient pattern.

5

5. "Maharam 'Repeat': Dots" for Maharam

The works establishes universality and relevancy in interior textile. The seamless and repeated patterns can make various unpredictable figures according to the different parts in use.

6. "Repeat Pillows" for Vitra

"Repeat" pillow series are used in her fabric works.

6

7. "Polder sofa" for Vitra

A sofa made with tapeling and embroidery technique. The fine detail and high quality make it a masterpiece in the collection of Vitra. The cushions in different sizes and subtle difference in the tone color are assembled well like a collage. The fasteners are made of nature materials such as horn, bamboo, pearl shell etc.

7

He studied Electric Engineering in Firenze College and studied Robot Engineering in Scuola Superiore Sant'Anna. He graduated in 1993.

In the same year, he began his career as an industrial designer and consultant. In 1995, he took part in the restructure project of building and residence. In 1994, he worked as professor in many universities in Europe and America. Now, he teaches architectural with digital system and computer. His latest researches are computer vision, semi–automatic robot, the interactivity of human and machine and application of multimedia system, etc.

Among his clients, there are a lot of famous makers who take Italy as beachhead such as Cappellini, Flexform, Poliform, Moroso, Ycami Edizioni and Zanotta. The chair "Fly2" and "Sintesi" furniture system published by Poliform on MILANO SALONE has been the subject of talk. Besides furniture design, he deals with interior design for residence and commercial buildings. He has stepped into various fields and become one of the most prominent designers.

As the leader of the second generation in the designing field of Italy, he has drawn great attention. He has been appraised as the contemporary representative.

Carlo Colombo
Born 1967 in Bari, Italy

The balance between beeline and curve is achieved through the calculation of architect. It looks like an artwork.

"EOS sfondo" for Nemo
The smooth surface radiates clean light.

Right: "BOLD" for Moroso
It is an excellent armchair with the perfect balance between metallic sharp frame and soft line.

1

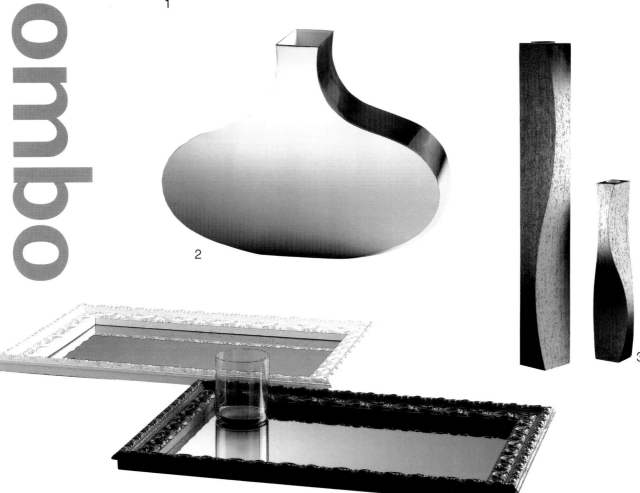

Carlo Colombo

2

3

4

5

1. "B-522-3.M" for Sabattini
Rococo candle stand in classical style.

2. "Sabattini" for Sabattini
A flower vase with perfect figure.

3. "B-507-9.W" for Sabattini
Uneven candle holder which looks like cortex.

4. "B-527B-M-N" for Sabattini
A tray with mirror appearance. The barpque frame creates elegant atmosphere.

5. "an36" for Zanotta
White dining set with fine line.

6. "Vasca Baia" for Antonio Lupi
Bathtub without compact shower system and excessive ornaments. The head shows complete simplicity.

6

1

215

He finished his architecture course in configuration research department of Graduate Faculty in Musashion Art University in 1994. In the second year, he started with construction design and founded INTENTIONALLIES with his college classmate. In order to arouse attention of the architects in the early 20th century, the INTENTIONALLIES with the objective of "creating future classicality in architecture" paid great attention to the integrated system of products, interior, landscape and house. They took the holistic harmony of the space into consideration. In 1996, he founded INTENTIONALLIES First-class Architect Office with the objective "completing one person's ten-year's work in three years by three persons".

They finished their first stage of work when the 'three years' is ended. INTENTIONALLIES started its second stage. They stepped into various fields from architecture to design such as hanamiduki, strasburgo, AGITO, kitchen atehaca, Face LCD, etc. They gave new life to HOTEL CLASKA—an old hotel which was built 35 years ago. It aroused great attention in Japan. TOSHIBA DYNABOOK CX1 series and Real Legs Model (limited in 500 sets) published in 2004 were very popular and sold out in 3 weeks. In 2002, he took part in the founding of Real Fleet and was appointed as creative director. In Real Fleet, he made a lot of brand designs for household appliances, which were more than Amadana. In 2005, he published world standard stationery brand "Craff Design Technology"and drew the attention worldwide for his future development.

Removing the barriers in the design of construction, furniture and interior decoration; targeting at future classicality.

Tei Syuwa
Born 1968 in Yokohama, Japan

Questioning the pursuit of spec, aiming at the PC with aesthetic attraction and tactile impression

"Dynabook"
Computer is an important tool. Can we design a kind of PC that makes people eager to use? The idea of the works came from that consideration. The case and keyboard are made of leather in the same color and they are easy to keep clean because of the fluorin processing technique. The production of this kind of PC is limited to 500 sets.

"Amadana"
These are the series of household electrical appliances. There are chairs, audio, shredder and humidifier.

1

2

1. Seaside Villa
A private beachfront house in Nugala of Bali Island, Indonesia. The area is 5500 m2. It takes the suggestion of Villa (the unique residence of the combination of the owner's house and hotel) as conception. The combination of the local materials with long history and the craftsman's fine work provide the furniture with direct tactile-impression.

2. "52.S-house"
It is a special building with the plot ratio of 8% in relation to the floor area of 1050 m2. The house is located at the versant which is not far from the incline zone of Haruna lake of Gunma County. A retired couple who moved from Tokyo lived in the house. They required for a simple house with the conception as described in the book-- Sermons of a Buddhist Abbot. The warm impression of fir floor, slope-shape side and the house seem to blend into the natural surroundings.

3. "Hotel Claska"
"Claska" is a proposal for the consideration of habitation. It is an old hotel built 35 years ago. However, after infused with the concept of living hotel, the hotel changed. Eight storeys are arranged into eight layers. The hotel revives. The materials used are widely available in Asia no matter in modern times or in old times. The materials all go through further processing. It is a perfect combination with Japanese traditional technique.

3

Björn Dahlström

In the middle time of 1970, he began to make animation graphics for movie and TV. As an art director and graphic designer, he worked for an advertisement company in 1978. In 1982, he founded his own company to deal with graphic design. He had clients such as Ericsson, Scania, Atlas Copco, etc. Now, 60% of his works are industrial designs. In this field, he had clients such as Primus, Atlas Copco, Aqua Play, Playsam, Gewa (electronical accessory for the handicapped), Skeppshult, Hackman, Magis, Plank, Zottan, etc.

In 1990s, he started several furniture projects. His main activities are designing CBI brands. He designed for the exhibitions and made animation videos. Besides, he taught in Beckmans Design School. As one of the industrial designers, he dealt with graphic design and product design for industry and furniture. In 1999, he was appointed as professor in Stockholm Art University. As a Sweden multidesigner, he stepped into many fields and he was highly appraised.

He attracts the world with simple and delicate design in mid-century style.

Björn Dahlström
Born 1957 in Stockholm, Sweden

A work that indicates the renovation of Swedish
design standard.

"BD Superstructure"
The arc–shaped strut across the center follows the traditional structure of Scandinavia shipbuilding. The
message is the revival of the Windsor style introduced from England to Sweden via Denmark. The message is shown by the spoke surrounding the strut. Though it's impossible to hide its novel style, there is
still something arouses the memory for the past. Moreover, the beautiful form of every angle is designed
with refined calculation.

Björn Dahlström

1

1. "BD Relax"

The relax chair is a combination of lounge and sleeping bag. It can be used out of the door. People who sit in the chair will feel warm and relaxed even in cold days. This idea can only come from the designers in North Europe.

2. "BD Lounge"

The lounge chair shows itself in the way of radiation and has the characteristics of pin base. The chair is made of oak triplex board.

3. "Pullover"

The stacking type chair with the legs which can be folded. It is notable for the balance between the warm seat which is made of fabric & oak and the sharp legs which are made of chromium materials.

2

3

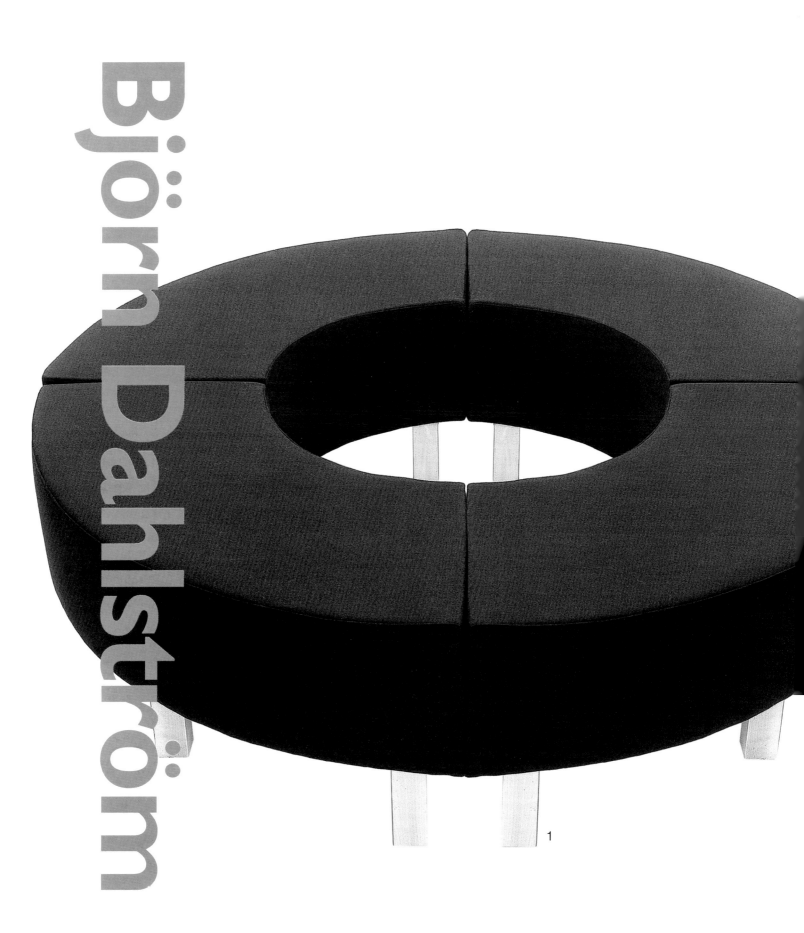

1

Björn Dahlström

2

1. "BD:4"
3. "BD:1"
The seat is made of high-consistency materials and polyurethane material. It is soft, firm and elastic. MDF is used on the base. It traces out pleasing unique curves. It is complete Swedish style.

2. "Soft Transport"
(boat / aeroplane)
The inspiration for the kids' toy came from vehicle.

3

Jasper Morrison

He studied Furniture Design in Royal College of Art. His excellent designs aroused attention when he was at the college and the designs were highly praised in the graduation exhibition. In 1986, he founded his own studio in London. In the same year, he designed plywood chair for the exhibition held in DAAD Gallery in Berlin. The fine design and good elasticity of the chair was highly praised. The delicate form, high performance, constructional simplicity and essence of humor became his style. The style attracted a lot of people and got a lot of support.

He became a world-class designer when his household interior designs were reported by media. In 1988, he took part in Berlin Design Werkstadt and published "Some new items for the home part I ". His early works are manufactured by Aram Dessigns, Cappellini, SCP Ltd in London, Neotu in Paris and FSB of German. In 1989, Vitra published "Some new items for the home part II " for him. Thereafter, he collaborated with some famous makers such as Alessi, Flos, Magis and Rosenthal in some projects. In 2000, he took part in the design of kitchen electric appliances for Rowenta.

In 1998, he was appointed as an instructor of design product in RCA. In 2001, he was chosen by Royal Designer for Industry to held Jasper Morrison Exhibition in Axis, Yamagiwa and HH Style in Tokyo. In 2004, he worked as consultant for Muji, Samsung and Ldeal Standard. As an authority on Interior Field, he is active on the world arena.

The sharp figure and good performance represent the peak level of minimalist, which cannot be imitated.

Jasper Morrison

Born 1959 in London, UK

The minimalism of Morrison gives us a symbolic view.

"Air Chair" for Magis
The raw material is polypropylene with fiberglass. It is made by air–molding technique. The delicate and soft lines as well as the color in pale tone embody the agile image of air. The small slot on the seat is used to drain water. Besides, it's convenient for you to put fingers into the slot to carry the chair.
©Walter Gumiero/Morrison Studio

1

2

1. "Oak Table Module" for Cappellini
Cute module system table. The tables are in different sizes. They can be used easily and arranged in many ways

2. "Soft Sim black" for Vitra
This work is the second generation of 'Sim' which was published formerly. The seat and backrest are made of textile stocking and the frame is made of chromium materials.

3

3. "Cork Family" for Vitra
Three lovely corks in different forms. They are the works that can be used as stools as well as side table. They bring the character of natural materials into full play. They are light, firm, comfortable and soft.

4. "Plate Coffee Tables" for Vitra
It is a classic table with the interleaving of soft curves and edges. It is made of white marble from Carrare, Italy. It is a kind of traditional material used from Renaissance Period.

4

Jasper Morrison

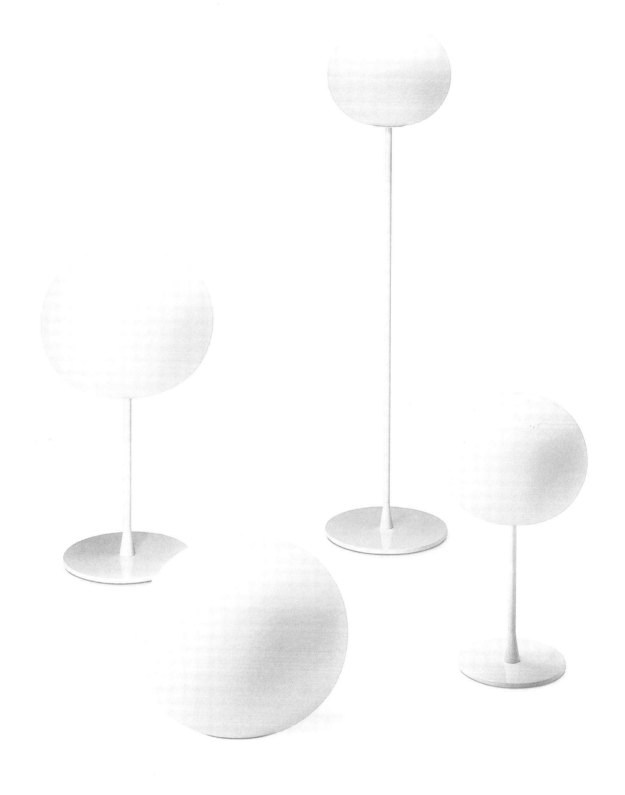

1

2

3

4

1. "Glo-Ball" for Flos

The big round sphere with light floating in the space shows unique coenesthesis in quietness.

2. Coffee Maker for Rowenta

It is contained in the same series of kettle. The necessary functions are contained though it is simple. It is practical.
©Christoph Kicherer

3. Knife Fork Spoon for Alessi

A cutlery design which can be considered as the perfection of simplicity.

4. Kettle for Rowenta

The designer is a master in Bauhaus. The simple form of the works embodies the concept of Bauhaus 'Form Follows Function'. The works won GOOD DESIGN Award 2004 in the CHICAGO ATHENAEUM.
©Christoph Kicherer

©Tom Whipps

He studied in Camondo Decoration Art College in Paris from 1966 to 1968. After graduation, he worked as art director for Pierre Cardin till 1972. His activity attracted the attention of the President Mitterrand and he dealt with the interior decoration work of private space in Elysee in 1982, when he was 33 years old. Thereafter, he made his mark in the design field. In 1984, he dealt with the interior decoration for CAFÉ COSTES in Paris. The chairs "COSTES" used there have been sold worldwide, and became one of his representative works.

In 1988, with the catalyst of Royal Ton in N.Y, he began interior design and furniture design for the hotels in many countries such as Paramount in N.Y, Peninsula in Hong Kong, Delano in Miami and Mondriaan in L.A. In 1989, he designed "Flamme d'O" for Asahi Breweries Ltd in Tokyo. This works became the No.1 of his construction design. Besides, in 1993, hc designed art gallery in Groningen in Holand with Michele De Lucchiand. It is highly praised. It is appraised as a masterpiece that "the building itself is one of the gallery's collections".

Now, he has the main clients such as Driade, Flos, Kartell, Vitra, etc. His outstanding ability and the activity with original idea spread throughout the designing field. Besides interior decoration and furniture design, he deals with the product designs such as Alessi tableware, Thomson household electrical appliances, Laguioe knife and Heller toilet brush.

He is a legendary man and the most famous French designer.

Philippe Starck

Born 1949 in Paris, France

Three–legged coffee chair designed for the famous café in Paris.

"Costes"/"King Costes" for Driade
The works was designed for the famous café "COSTES" in Pairs les halles area in 1982. It is his early representative works (left of the picture). Compared with Anton chair—the representative three–legged chair, it is designed to prevent the waiter from tripping. Its width is 47cm, but the unique curved backrest and elastic leather cushion make people comfortable when sitting. Considering stability, the four–legged type is adopted by "King Costes".

Philippe Starck

1

2

1. "Lago' " for Driade
An armchair with the balance of the round seat and sharp legs. The seat is made of hard polyurethane and leather. The legs are made of aluminum materials. They displayed in two versions.

2. "Lord YO" for Driade
As a basic product, it is popular with a lot of people and it is one of his representative chairs. It has smooth curve. It is made by advanced resin molding technique.

3. "Mademoisselle (Missoni)" for Kartell
The transparent legs which are made of polycarbonate material; the sofa seat which covered with fabric; the four coupling points and the softness of the urethane material embody the combination of high-performance and aesthetic attraction. The curved shape of the armrest is designed for folding the chair and putting it under the table.

4. "Victoria Ghost" for Kartell
A chair consists of classical ellipse backrest and simple shape with the feature of geometry which shows the refined atmosphere. It is made of polycarbonate materials.

3

4

Philippe Starck

1

236

2

3

1. "Royal T" for Kartell
A stool with helicoid figure can show various shapes. Plastics can create such smooth curve. It's really a challenge to the imagination of human being.

2. "Lola Mundo" for Driade
Furniture in the style of classic antique. The stainless steel is used in the works to show elegance.

3. "Jelly Slice" for Driade
From its name, we know that it is the table series made of board like jelly slice. There are yellow glass and white glass. The yellow type is painting yellow color on the underside of the glass sheet. The color will vary from deep green to fresh yellow according to different perspective.

Philippe Starck

1

2

3

238

4

1. "Collection La Vie" for Flos
The desk lamp which offers a kind of irony to the world where people are crazy about money and stock.

2. "Collection Guns" for Flos
A floor lamp which condemns war and terrorism.

3. "Neoz" series for Driade
The series of works are made in the way of adding unique irony to French noble interest and arranging it to modern style. It is designed to cover all the basic space such as living room, dining room and bedroom. The mixed fabric of high-quality linen and cotton is used to make the covering. Besides, the table is made of marble.

4. "Delano Hotel" in Miami, USA
A resort hotel located in the center of Art Deco on the beach of Miami. It is built in 1974 first. It is named after the middle name of the president—Rooservelt. It is built by Starck. The white appearance and interior decoration is his main features.

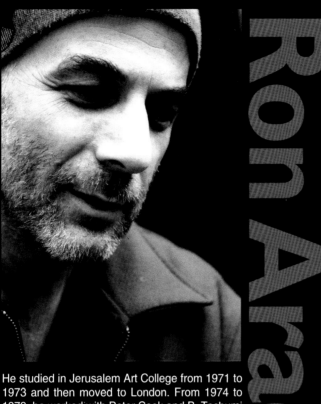

Ron Arad

He studied in Jerusalem Art College from 1971 to 1973 and then moved to London. From 1974 to 1979, he worked with Peter Cook and B. Tschumi for London Architecture Association. In 1981, he founded design studio One Off with Caroline Thorman. In 1983, he founded a showroom. He made his mark in Interior Field with Rover seat and the chair "ROVER CHAIR" which was made of iron pipe. In 1989, he founded Ron Arad Associates, Ltd—an architecture design office and designed for the world top-ranking makers such as Vitra, poltronova etc. Besides, he dealt with construction and interior design of café, restaurant, gallery and Tel Aviv Operahouse in London, Mialno, Berlin and France. In 1994, he founded Ron Arad Studio in Como, Italy. His exploration to new materials, new techniques and engineer aroused attention of the world. From 1994 to 1997, he worked as a professor of product design in Hochschule College in Wien. In 1997, he taught in a design college in London. In that college, his uncommon subject "design for the improvement of homeless life" amazed his students.

He drew great attention in Milano Salone these years. Especially in 2000, his experimental works such as helical luminaire became known to public. At present, he is attempting at new carving techniques such as using iron board, curving wood for leg-making and combination board. Meanwhile, a sculptor and craftsman, he continues producing beautiful and practical furniture with esthetic attraction.

A great designer who continues to conquer the age.

Ron Arad
Born 1951 in Tel Aviv, Israel

A ripple chair which give people strong impact. You will never forget it after the first sight.

"Ripple Chair" for Moroso
No matter for him or for Moroso Company, it is the work that is considered as icon chair. Its simple form and elegant figure which looks like a butterfly leave people deep impression. The frame is made of white glazing technique (picture is unavailable) which is similar to thermoplastic injection molding technique. The works features the round holes on the seat, smooth line, firm material (polypropylene) and stackable characteristics. The chair can be used both in the house and public place

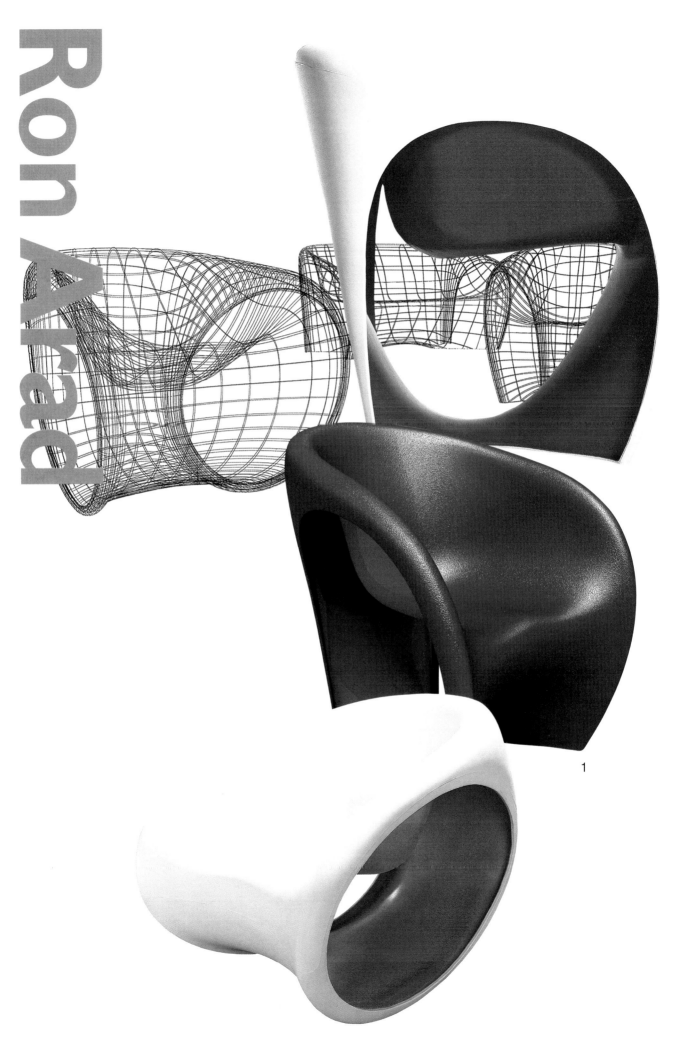

Ron Arad

1

242

1. "MT 3" for Driade
One of the MT series. It consists of armchair, sofa and rocking chair. The unique form is made with rotational molding technique. After the inside and outside are painted, chair will be hollowed from out from the sides. The material of this works is polyethylene. The name of this works came out because that the pronunciation of "MT" is similar to "empty".

2. "Bloo Void"
One of the Paperwork Collections. It can be regarded as the prototype of his rocking chair.

3. "Paperwark 3 Skin Joint"
©Tom Vack

4. "Screw" for Driade
On the mirror-like aluminum base is winded by the satin stainless steel. The seat and footrest are made of the satin stainless steel. The helical base gives people a strong sense of impact. Besides, the height can be adjusted according by corcwing.

2

3

4

Ron Arad

1

2

244

1. "Lo-Rez-Dolores-Tabula-Rasa" in NY

A project installation of dupont-corian of MRC dupont is adopted. As the designer wants to display art with low-resolution picture, the theme of this project is 'low resolution'. The big screen is made of white thin corian sheets; a lot of optical fibers are set in the holes in the screens to reflect the pictures. Besides, with the hint of the shape of chocolate and M&M, there is a bird flapping its wings in the ellipse table.

2. "Lolita" for Swarovski at Venice Biennale

This crystal chandelier is used by Swarovsk Company. This work expresses the text delivered by E-mail with the helical chandelier. It is interactive and artful.

3. "Y's Store" in Tokyo

Y's Store opened in Oppongi Hills in 2003. He was entrusted by the stock-holding company Yohji Yamamoto to work as designer and project designer. He dealt with the design and interior decoration. The inspiration of the helical hanger rack came from the turn table of the cubic parking space in Tokyo. The rack is made of 34 aluminum tubes. It is called movcable sculpture.

3

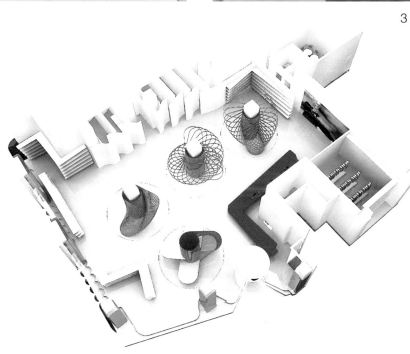

1

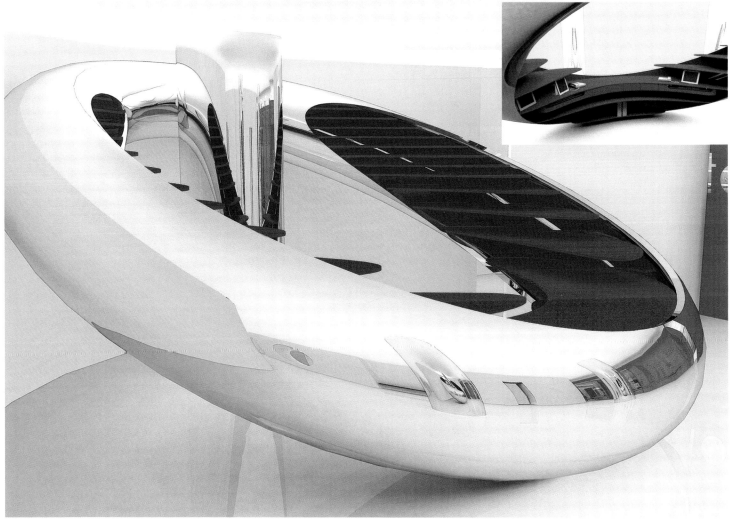

1. "Hotel Duomo" in Rimini

A hotel located at the resort of Adriatic Sea. A bar and a club are in the middle of the hotel. The bronze and stainless steel decoration in the interior show a kind of overwhelming coenesthesis. Besides, the round reception made of stainless steel is amazing. The hotel opened in the early summer of 2006.

2. "Hotel Puerta America" in Madrid

A 14-storey hotel designed by 14 designers, each designer for one floor. Separating the room with a wall in the middle, the bedroom, bathroom, dressing area and study room are formed. A luxurious detail is set to form undulant space.

2

©Antonio Citterio & Partners

Antonio Citterio's father is a furniture craftsman; so, he was bent on becoming a designer even when he cut his wisdom teeth and he studied design when he was 13 years old. In 1972, he graduated from Architecture Department of Milano Engineering University. In the same year, he founded a studio and worked as a designer and a consultant to deal with industrial design. In 1981, he began his career of architecture and interior design.

He has a lot of clients such as Ansorg, Arclinea, Axor-Hansgorhe, B&B Italia, Flexform, Flos, Fusital, Guzzini, Iittala, Kartell, Maxalto and Vitra. He published many splendid works, among which 'Mobil system' and "battista" became the permanent collections of MOMA. He won the prize of "Compasso d'oro" twice respectively in 1987 and 1985.

In 1987, he founded Studio--Citterio Dwan with Terry Dwan, his partner. In 1999, he founded Antonio Citterio & Partners with Patricia. From then on, he began to deal with architecture design, industrial design and graphic design. He designed many main facilities such as apartment complex, trading centre, industrial land, public construction, offices, showroom and hotel. His main projects were showroom and office for Vitra, Branch of Commercial Bank for German, No.1 line of subway in Milano and the reconstruction of A line of the subway in Roma.In order to learn architecture, he traveled all over the world and saw the works of Le Corbusier, Tadao Ando and other designers. He thinks much of the relationship between design and the space when designing products. He holds that as a designer, he should observe space with a full vision to reach the harmony between the nature of the object and the function users expected on the object. In this way, the object can perform its function of improving the life quality of human beings very well.

From architecture to product design, he is a great Italian modern designer who leads the trend of Interior Field.

Antonio Citterio
Born 1950 in Meda, Italy

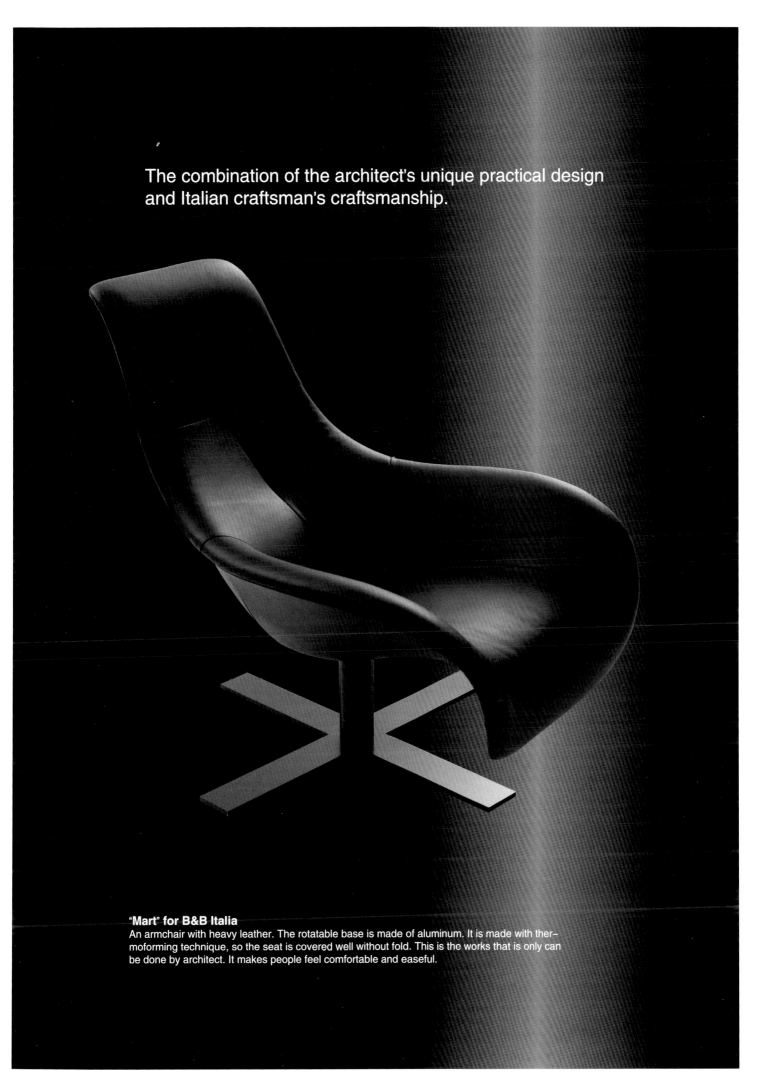

The combination of the architect's unique practical design and Italian craftsman's craftsmanship.

"Mart" for B&B Italia
An armchair with heavy leather. The rotatable base is made of aluminum. It is made with ther-moforming technique, so the seat is covered well without fold. This is the works that is only can be done by architect. It makes people feel comfortable and easeful.

1

2

3

1. "Ad Hoc" office system for Vitra

This is one works of office system series published by Vitra. The ceiling without dead space can match up with the space under the table of each cabinet. It's simple, but with high performance given by the detailed calculation.
©Antonio Citterio & Partners

2. "Flip" for Kartell

A side table with casters. It is designed jointly by him and Toan Nguyen. The slim figure is very elegant.
©Kartell

4

3. "Spoon Chair" for Kartell

This is also designed by him and Toan Nguyen. It is a chair edition of 'Spoon Stool' which is published before. The lovely curve is its special feature.
©Kartell

4. "My Table" cutlery for Fratelli Guzzini

My table series is one part of his cutlery designs. The name of the works shows that the simple work is suitable for daily use. However, it holds the elegant figure.
©Kartell

5

5. "J.J" chair for B&B

A chair with small armrests. It is published after Arne system. There are two sizes; a high backrest is set on the bigger type for relaxing. The type with lower backrest is designed for people to talk. The frame is made of oak materials. The frame can fit in with your back. The seat is made of cowskin or pony skin.
©Antonio Citterio & Partners

6

6. "Arne" sofa system for B&B

An arch-shaped sofa with different depth according to the part you sit. The armrest has two different types. One is curve-shaped; the other one is high and barrel-shaped. So the ends are easy to be separated out. It is an innovative idea to the sofa. The two people sitting on the two ends can talk while looking at each other.

1

1. "Antonio Citterio and Partners' studio" in Milano, Italy

Antonio Citterio and Partners' studio in Milano. The glass is so eye-catching among the crowded stone buildings.

©Antonio Citterio & Partners

2. "Edel Musica Headquarters" in Hamburg, Germany

The new head office building of Edel music AG. It faces Elbe River of Hamburg. The building is similar to the campus. Reception, bar, restaurant and lecture room are set on the ground floor. The clerks of the company can communicate with the visitors from all over the world and the youths have chance to meet the people who work there.

©Antonio Citterio & Partners

3. "Bulgari Hotel Milano" in Italy

Reconstructing the building of 1950 is the first step for him to enter the hotel field of Bulgari Group. The facade of the building is decorated with white marble so as to make the windows more noticeable. Black bronze is used as keynote in the inside and helpful to create a sweet and pleasing atmosphere.

©Antonio Citterio & Partners

INDEX

A

Afke Golsteijn	112
Alfredo Haberli	198
Antonio Citterio	248
Arik Levy	034

B

Björn Dahlström	220

C

Carlo Colombo	210
Chris Kabel	090
Claesson Koivisto Rune	178
COMMITTEE	096

D

defyra	130
Design Dessert	126
5.5 designers	100

E

Emiko Oki	106
Eric Gizard	058

F

Fernando+Humberto Campapna	150
Frank Tjepkema	072

H

Hella Jongerius	206

I

India Mahdavi	054
Ineke Hans	082

J

Jasper Morrison	226
Jean-Marie Massaud	050
Johannes Norlander	046
Joris Laarman	068

K

Koichiro Kimura	078

L

Laurent Massaloux	064

M

Maarten Baas	022
Marcel Wanders	170
Monica Förster	132

N

Nendo	086

P

Patricia Urquiola	162
Pernilla Jansson	124
Philippe Starck	232
Piet Hein Eek	016

R

Ronan & Erwan Bouroullec	190
Ron Arad	240

S

Simon Heijdens	030
Stuart Haygarth	098
STUDIO JOB	006

T

Ted Noten	118
Tei Syuwa	216
Thomas Bernstrand	138
Todd Bracher	142
Tom Dixon	154

W

Wataru Komachi	120
Wieki Somers	108

Y

Yves Béhar	044

Data Source/Enquiry Place

hhstyle.com harajiku Head Office
6-14-2, Jingumae, Shibuya-Ku, Tokyo
TEL:03-3400-3434
P198   Alfredo Haberli
Nais(P199)

Kartell shop aoyama
2F, COLLEZIONE, 6-1-3, Minami Aoyama, Minato-Ku, Tokyo
TEL:03-5468-2328
P232   Philippe Starck
Victoria Ghost(P235)、Mademoisselle(P235)

CIBONE AOYAMA
B1 , Bell Commons Aoyama, 2-14-6, Kita Aokaya, Minato Ku, Tokyo
TEL: 03-3408-2578
P006   STUDIO JOB
P016   Piet Hein Eek
P022   Maarten Baas
P096   COMMITTEE
P098   Stuart Haygarth
P108   Wieki Somers
Hight Tea Pot (P109)
P120   Wataru Komachi
P170   Marcel Wanders
Products for moooi

Da driade aoyama
3-16-3, Minami Aoyama, Minato-Ku, Tokyo
TEL:03-5770-1511(representative office)
P162   Patricia Urquiola
Flo(P165)、Pavo(P165)
P226   Jasper Morrison
Air Chair (P227) 、Glo-Ball (P229) 、Kettle、CoffeeMaker(P229)
P232   Philippe Starck
Costes(P233) 、Jelly Slice(P237) 、Lola Mundo(P237) 、Neoz(P239) 、
P240 Ron Arad
MT3(P243)

PG Gallery
1-15-5, Higashiyama, Meguro-Ku, Tokyo
TEL:03-5725-1701
P220   Björn Dahlström